THE BEST OF HOLY DAYS & HOLIDAYS

THE BEST OF
HOLY DAYS
& HOLIDAYS

Prayer Celebrations With Children

GAYNELL BORDES CRONIN

ST. ANTHONY MESSENGER PRESS
AND FRANCISCAN COMMUNICATIONS

Cincinnati, Ohio

Permission is granted to purchasers of *The Best of Holy Days and Holidays: Prayer Celebrations With Children* to reproduce the prayer celebrations in this book for family or student use.

Scripture citations are taken from several sources: *The Good News Bible, Old Testament,* copyright ©1976 American Bible Society; *The Good News Bible, New Testament,* copyright ©1966, 1971, 1976, American Bible Society; *Revised Standard Version of the Bible,* copyright ©1946, 1952, 1971, by the Division of Christian Education of the National Council of the Churches of Christ in the USA, and are used by permission.

Cover illustration by Ursula Roma/Little Bear Graphics
Cover design by Mary Alfieri
Book illustrations by Chris Larson and Katherine Tillotson/Imprint

ISBN 0-86716-278-3

Copyright ©1997, Gaynell Bordes Cronin

Published by St. Anthony Messenger Press/Franciscan Communications
Printed in the U.S.A.

Contents

Introduction

Every Mardi Gras day, after the last carnival parade in New Orleans, we went to Grandma's house. I never knew which I enjoyed more—the parades or Grandma's homemade *beignets* (fried French doughnuts covered with powdered sugar). Regardless of our age, we were allowed to drink Grandma's chickory coffee with boiled milk. The smell and taste of those *beignets* and chickory still linger, and the memory of gathering with aunts, uncles and cousins awakens my feelings of what it means to belong to and be a family.

We all have grandmas in our lives. They are the people who provide a place for gathering, who welcome others with open hearts, who create an environment of belonging, who use the gifts of creation to celebrate God's presence, who make space sacred. And we are all invited to be grandmas for others, to welcome and gather into our space at all times and places all the people of north, south, east and west of long ago, today and those yet to be.

In making space sacred, we let it become a dwelling place for a journeying people—a place to give focus, a place to mark in ritual who we are and who we are called to be. With gestures and signs, words and movements, we celebrate the seasons of our lives, the seasons of the natural world, the seasons of our hearts.

In 1978, as a mother of four children, a catechist and director of religious education, I wanted to pass on the gift of faith experienced and expressed by my parents, teachers, relatives and especially my grandmother. It wasn't just Mardi Gras day that we went to Grandma's house; every Sunday my family gathered there, told stories, ate, played, prayed and celebrated.

These were joyous and peace-filled times when I learned what it meant to listen, remember, enjoy and be healed by the power of families as home churches. Because I wanted my growing family and students to experience this companioning God within and among us, we started to create simple celebrations and rituals for our home and family. These prayer celebrations were contained in *Holy Days and Holidays: Prayer Celebrations With Children*. This book followed the calendar and was welcomed and used by families, catechists and parish staffs in classrooms and churches. Volunteer catechists found *Holy Days and Holidays* easy to follow; parochial school teachers used these prayer celebrations for their classes and weekly church gatherings. In this book it was suggested that a symbol for each celebration be placed on a banner under the words, "Celebrating God Throughout the Year." The banner became a way to summarize the events in which we had tried to recognize God's presence.

Ten years later, with children entering adulthood and planning to start their own families, *Holy Days and Holidays Volume II* emerged. Following the same basic format as the first volume, it contained many more cross-cultural feasts and challenged believers to see themselves as a part of a much larger whole. Using creation as a guide, it incorporated all the same elements of song, body movement and sacred gesture in more elaborate celebrations. It, too, was widely used in classrooms and parish churches. In that book, four colors represented the four seasons of the year—blue for winter, yellow for summer, green for spring, orange for autumn. We suggested that people display in the area used for rituals and celebrations a simple panel of cloth or other material in the chosen color during the appropriate season. The changing panels for each season were visual reminders that we are a growing and journeying people seeking to be in touch with all the seasons of our lives. This suggestion to display colored panels appears also in the celebrations chosen from *Holy Days and Holidays II* for this latest volume, *The Best of Holydays and Holidays: Prayer Celebrations With Children.*

Now it is 1996. Still a mother, I am also a grandmother and friend to my own adult children and feel deeply the same passion to hand on to them and my grandchildren the joyful faith that my grandmother shared with me. Hence, *The Best of Holy Days and Holidays* combines the most often used celebrations found in the first two volumes. This book contains twenty-four days and events to celebrate. For each day you will find a Background Reflection, Preparation, Project and Prayer Celebration. Each prayer celebration centers around four parts: opening greeting, reading(s), an exchange specific to the day, and a closing prayer or blessing. If the children are young, select only one or two parts of the four-part service. Copies of the Prayer Celebration are not necessary for the participants because any response asked for will always be given by the leader or reader.

The same format for this new book was used in both of the earlier volumes of *Holy Days and Holidays*. But because prayer celebrations for this current volume were compiled from two previous volumes, you will note a difference in the length of the prayer services and the suggestion of a colored panel for the season for those celebrations that were originally published in the second volume. Many of the prayer celebrations, for example, Good Friday, Harvest Day, World Peace Day, Earth Day, lend themselves to large gatherings. We have used them for sacramental preparation programs for parents, teachers, candidates.

In discovering their own inherent "grandma," catechists have provided a welcoming and safe environment for their students to express through ritual and symbols their longing for God and God for them. The catechists' gentle invitation to enter into the mystery of God, their respect and reverence for the gifts of others and creation, and their deep conviction through the experience of sharing and passing on one's faith through ritual celebration has renewed many of us. These men and women, often parents themselves, accept their families as home churches in all their fragility and weakness. Because of the requests of these people and St. Anthony Messenger Press, this book, *The Best of Holy Days and Holidays: Prayer Celebrations With Children*, emerged.

Gestures and signs, words and movement call not only for active involvement and participation in these celebrations, but speak to what we carry inside us as a people and connect us to our past, present and future. Through celebrations, we get a glimpse into the mystery of God, the mystery of self and the mystery of who we are as a people, and thus we are nourished for daily living. Too often we reduce the formal expressions of religious faith to only the spoken word. That is, I fear, a tragic mistake. When believers sing, dance, process and enter into the mystery of ritual prayer, we are able to experience the depth of God's unconditional love for us and the challenge to pass it on. God is intimately present in all creation, dwelling within and among all of us. We simply need eyes that see and hearts that listen to recognize that presence. We need our deepest inside selves awakened and delighted through the celebration of that presence. And we need to do it together, as one people of God, brothers and sisters in a gathered family.

It is my hope that those who use this book will touch the creative side of themselves and learn how to create their own celebrations and prayers. When believers think of God as entering our lives only at those sacred moments we spend together in churches, we cheat ourselves of the God who is always among us, beckoning us with every breath we take to enter the mystery of the divine presence and love.

So, pick a leader, select the theme, choose which elements of the prayer celebration best suit your class, family or parish group, and then celebrate the wondrous gifts of faith in a thousand different ways. Hear God's call and allow yourself the privilege of being "grandma" to others.

Gaynell Bordes Cronin
Epiphany 1997

Christian Unity Week

A Background Reflection

Many Christian churches devote eight days, usually beginning January 18 and ending January 25, to praying for unity among all Christian churches. This is a time to reflect and remember Jesus' words, "I pray that they may all be one" (John 17:21).

Many communities hold an interfaith prayer service as a sign of their common faith in Christ and in their shared responsibility to care for all people. Sometimes we are strangers even to ourselves and make strangers of family members, of work associates, of others in our nation. This week of prayer offers us an opportunity to reach out to others so that we ". . . are not foreigners or strangers any longer" (Ephesians 2:19).

Begun by the Graymoor Fathers, this celebration of ecumenical committment is sponsored by the Faith and Order Commission of the World Council of Churches and the Secretariat for Promoting Christian Unity of the Vatican and in the United States by the Faith and Order Commission of the National Council and the National Conference of Catholic Bishops' Committee on Ecumenical and Interreligious Affairs. Materials and services for this week of prayer continue to be published by Graymoor, Garrison, N.Y. 10524.

If it is not possible to gather together for an interfaith service, pray together as a family or class. This week of prayer is an excellent opportunity to celebrate and begin to live Jesus' prayer of oneness. During the Week of Prayer for Christian Unity, let us accept our differences and recognize ourselves as the family of God.

Preparation

directions

Complete the projects.

Choose a leader and five readers.

Practice singing "Let There Be Peace on Earth" or another appropriate song.

Gather the participants, wearing their symbols, in a circle. Place the chain of unity on the floor in the middle of the circle.

materials

construction paper in a variety of colors
scissors
paste or glue
pins

Projects

Have the participants make a brightly-colored construction-paper chain of unity.

Have each participant choose and make one of the symbols of Jesus shown below to wear during the celebration.

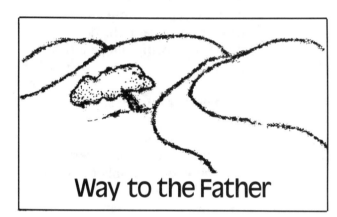

Way to the Father

Light of the World

Good Shepherd

Bread of Life

Prayer Celebration

Introduction

LEADER: Today we celebrate our call to be God's people. Because we believe in Jesus, we are not strangers to each other. Though we may belong to different churches, our faith in Jesus makes us one.

READER 1: The blood of Jesus has brought you near, even though you were once far away. It's because of him that we have peace and unity, instead of the discord we used to have. Through him, we go to the Father. You are outsiders no longer. You belong to the house of God.

(adapted from Ephesians 2:13-14, 18-19)

Prayers of Petition

LEADER: Sometimes we are strangers to ourselves. We are lonely; we are afraid to love ourselves.

ALL: Help us, Lord, to be strangers no longer.

LEADER: Sometimes we are strangers to our families. We hide our feelings of love and do not help those who are hurting.

ALL: Help us, Lord, to be strangers no longer.

LEADER: Sometimes we are strangers to other families. We forget to pray for orphaned children, for broken homes, for lonely, neglected parents and grandparents.

ALL: Help us, Lord, to be strangers no longer.

LEADER: Sometimes we are strangers to our community. We turn away from neighbors of a different race, culture, or religion. We forget the handicapped. Sometimes we do not even know the people next door.

ALL: Help us, Lord, to be strangers no longer.

LEADER: Sometimes we are strangers in our work. We forget the unemployed, or those whose work is hard and dull. We forget the joy of doing a job well.

ALL: Help us, Lord, to be strangers no longer.

LEADER: Sometimes we are strangers in our churches, not only our own church but the different churches in our community. We forget to respect and seek out from them the truths that they hold.

ALL: Help us, Lord, to be strangers no longer.

LEADER: God, our Father, thank you for sending Jesus. Help us obey your call in showing unity in your church. Amen.

Ceremony of Unity

LEADER: We have been made one in Christ. Each of us wears a different sign of Jesus. As your sign is named, come forward and stand close to our chain of unity.

READER 2: And Jesus said, "I am the way, the truth, and the life. No one goes to the Father unless he goes through me. Now that you have known me, you will know my Father, also."

(adapted from John 14:6)

LEADER: Come forward, you who follow the way of Christ.

(Participants wearing Way-to-the-Father symbols come forward.)

READER 3: And Jesus said, "I am the light of the world. No one who follows me will live in the dark. No, they shall have the light of life."

(adapted from John 8:12)

LEADER: Come forward, you who follow the light of Christ.

(Participants wearing Light-of-the-World symbols come forward.)

READER 4: Jesus told his followers that he was the Good Shepherd. He said, "I know every one of my sheep, and each one of them knows me, just as the Father and I know each other. Some day there will be only one flock and one shepherd."

(adapted from John 10:14-16)

LEADER: Come forward, you who follow Jesus as the Good Shepherd.

(Participants wearing Good-Shepherd symbols come forward.)

READER 5: And Jesus said, "I am the bread of life. Those who come to me shall not go away hungry and those who believe in me shall not be thirsty."

(adapted from John 6:35)

LEADER: Come forward, you who follow Jesus as the bread of life.

(Participants wearing Bread-of-Life symbols come forward.)

To show that we are one, that we are no longer strangers to each other, let us greet the persons near us in the chain and offer them the peace of Christ.

(Participants exchange greetings.)

Concluding Rite

LEADER: Let us hold the chain of unity and together pray the way Jesus taught us.

ALL: Our Father, who art in heaven....

LEADER: Let us sing our closing song together.

ALL: (Sing "Let There Be Peace on Earth" or another appropriate song.)

Martin Luther King Day

A Background Reflection

Only four people in U.S. history have been honored with national holidays: Christopher Columbus, George Washington, Abraham Lincoln, and now civil rights leader Martin Luther King, Jr. The Federal Holiday Commission in 1986 honored the birth of King on January 20 by asking Americans to pledge themselves to make the world a place where equality and justice, freedom and peace would grow and flourish. People were asked to commit themselves to living the dream by

> Loving, not hating,
> Showing understanding, not anger,
> Making peace, not war.

This twentieth day of January can become a time for rededicating ourselves to the goal of equal rights for all Americans and a day to honor the most famous southerner of our twentieth century.

But who is this man who cherished racial and religious diversity, who saw the civil rights revolution not as a black rebellion but as a covenant of white and black, Christian and Jews, standing together for decency. A winner of the Nobel Peace Prize, King was deeply influenced by the teachings of Mohandas Gandhi (the famous civil rights leader in India) and was committed to nonviolence in his pursuit of social justice for black Americans.

Who is this man called by some the "conscience of the nation" and by others the "apostle of nonviolence"? Many people speak of a profound bond of mutual respect, and a deep sense of solidarity with the mission of King. Perhaps they feel thus because King's goal was not only justice for America's blacks but human rights for all people and peace everywhere. His challenge to us is to share a vision of a compassionate and open society.

The son of a pastor and a school teacher, King grew up in Atlanta, Georgia, and was ordained a Baptist minister. While serving as a pastor in Montgomery, Alabama, he led a bus boycott that lasted more than a year but ended in the desegregation of buses. Rosa Parks, a black seamstress who refused to relinquish her seat to a white man, triggered this bus boycott. Of Parks, King later wrote, "She was anchored to that seat by the accumulated indignities of days gone by and the boundless aspirations of generations yet unborn."

After this successful bus boycott, King and his followers saw the need for similar efforts throughout the South. Together, they organized the Southern Christian Leadership Conference (SCLC) and struggled throughout the late 1950s and 1960s to end segregation and racism in the United States. In Birmingham, Alabama, King led mass demonstrations to protest segregation of public facilities. Here he was arrested and while in solitary confinement wrote his famous "Letter from the Birmingham Jail," which set forth his theory of nonviolent civil disobedience.

Throughout his life King's philosophy remained the same: to meet the forces of hate with the power of love, to forgive your enemies, and to use no violence. Even though he, his family, and the entire civil rights movement was increasingly plagued by violence, King never lost his faith in nonviolence or in the essential decency of people, black and white. Climaxing in the historic march on Washington in August 1963, King addressed 250,000 demonstrators gathered at the Lincoln Memorial in a speech that came to epitomize the man and his struggle:

> Even though we face the difficulties of today and tomorrow, I still have a dream. I have a dream that one day this nation will rise up and live out the true meaning of its creed, "we hold these truths to be self-evident, that all people are created equal."

As with all men and women who deepen their understanding of what it is to be brothers and sisters made in the image and likeness of God, King's compassion for the victims of prejudice extended to poor people so that they too could claim their share of the American promise. He also spoke out against the war in Vietnam because he believed that peace and freedom could not be separated.

While in Memphis, Tennessee, supporting sanitation workers who were striking for better wages and working conditions, King was murdered by an assassin's bullet. The day before his funeral, his wife, Coretta Scott King, after leading a silent memorial march with her three oldest children through Memphis, addressed the crowd at City Hall with these words:

We must carry on because this is the way he would have wanted it to have been. We are going to continue his work to make all people truly free and to make every person feel that he or she is a human being.

Like Martin Luther King, Jr., we are challenged to share in the life of the poor and oppressed as we work for social justice and as we deepen our understanding through the words of Paul in Scripture that we are all children of God, we are one.

So God does not see you as Jew or Greek. God does not see you as slave or free. God does not see you as man or woman. There are no differences among you. You are all one in Jesus.

Galatians 3:26–28 (adapted)

Preparations

directions

Use the blue panel (for winter) as a cloth to spread on a gathering table. Place the project words "Our Dream" down the middle of the table.   Distribute placemats around the table.

Place a candle to represent the Dream Candle of Peace on the table.

Choose six readers.

Alert participants that they will be sharing the symbol they have made on their placemats.

materials

Candle
Colored paper
Scissors and crayons/magic markers
A table

Project

Make the words "Our Dream" for the center of the table (draw, paint, cut out, or so on).

Cut out 11 × 18-inch placemats from colored construction paper. Participants decorate their placemats with their names, symbols of the work they do, and their dreams of who we are and what we can be as a people.

Prayer Celebration

Opening Greeting

LEADER: Welcome to a day of celebration, a day of remembering the dreams of Martin Luther King, Jr., a day of pledging ourselves to loving, not hating; showing understanding, not anger; making peace, not war. Lord, we are your people. You have made each of us in your own image and likeness. As we light our Dream Candle of Peace, we ask for hands and hearts that will help build a world where equality and justice, freedom and peace, will grow and flourish.

The peace of the Lord be with you.

ALL: And also with you.

The Readings

LEADER: Paul had a dream in which all people could live together as one. It is through Jesus that we know how deeply God loves all of us. This is what Paul told the people of Galatia.

READER 1: "Now that you have put your trust in Jesus, you are children of God. God does not see you as Jew or Greek. God does not see you as a slave or a free person. God does not see you as a man or a woman. There are no differences among you. You are all one in Jesus. If you belong to Jesus, you are truly children of Abraham our Father. What was promised Abraham, God will give to you, too."

Galatians 3:26–29 (adapted)

This is the Word of the Lord.

ALL: Thanks be to God.

LEADER: Martin Luther King, Jr., had that same dream as Paul. One day at the Lincoln Memorial in Washington, D.C., he spoke of this dream to all of us.

READER 2: "I say to you today, my friends, even though we face the difficulties of today and tomorrow, I still have a dream. It is a dream deeply rooted in the American dream. I have a dream that one day this nation will rise up and live out the true meaning of its creed: 'We hold these truths to be self-evident, that all people are created equal.'"

LEADER: What is the one difficulty that you face today?

(pause)

What self-evident truth is part of your creed?

READER 3: "I have a dream that one day on the red hills of Georgia the sons and daughters of former slaves and the sons and daughters of former slaveowners will be able to sit down together at the table of brotherhood and sisterhood. I have a dream that my four little children will one day live in a nation where they will not be judged by the color of their skin, but by the content of their character."

LEADER: Whom would you find difficult to invite to sit down at your table?

(pause)

How do you feel when you are judged by others? How do you judge others?

(pause)

READER 4: "I have a dream that one day every valley shall be exalted, every hill and mountain shall be made low, the rough places will be made plain, and the crooked places will be made straight, and the glory of the Lord shall be revealed, and all flesh shall see it together."

LEADER: What rough places are you making smooth?

(pause)

What crooked places are you making straight?

(pause)

READER 5: "When we allow freedom to ring — when we let it ring from every city and every hamlet, from every state and every city, we will be able to speed up that day when all of God's children, black and white, Jews and Gentiles, Protestants and Catholics, will be able to join hands and sing in the words of the old spiritual, 'Free at last, Free at last, Great God Almighty, we are free at last!'"

LEADER: What keeps you in your own kind of slavery?

(pause)

Who helps you to become free?

(pause)

The Freedom Litany

LEADER: People have spoken of freedom down through the centuries. They lived their lives with the dream of one day gathering together as one in the name of God. We give thanks for these dream makers and dream keepers. For Moses, who brought a people across the desert from slavery to freedom, so that one day we will say together, "Free at last, free at last!"

ALL: Free at last, free at last!

LEADER: For prophets Isaiah and John the Baptist who helped the people remember the dream so that one day we will say together, "Free at last, free at last!"

ALL: Free at last, free at last!

LEADER: For Mary who taught Jesus the dreams of his people so that one day we will say together, "Free at last, free at last!"

ALL: Free at last, free at last!

LEADER: For Frederick Douglass, who wrote and spoke against slavery, so that one day we will say together, "Free at last, free at last!"

ALL: Free at last, free at last!

LEADER: For Harriet Tubman, who helped escaped slaves reach freedom through the underground railroads, so that one day we will say together, 'Free at last, free at last!"

ALL: Free at last, free at last!

LEADER: For Mary McLeod Bethune, who founded a college to help improve social and educational opportunities for blacks, so that one day we will say together, "Free at last, free at last!"

ALL: Free at last, free at last!

LEADER: For Rosa Parks, a black seamstress who refused to give her bus seat to a white person, so that one day we will say together, "Free at last, free at last!"

ALL: Free at last, free at last!

LEADER: For Martin Luther King, Jr., a Baptist minister who struggled for the rights of black people and the poor to share in the promise of America, so that one day we will say together, "Free at last, free at last!"

ALL: Free at last, free at last!

LEADER: For each of us who strive for the recognition of human rights for all people around the planet Earth, so that one day we will say together, "Free at last, free at last!"

ALL: Free at last, free at last!

LEADER: Lord, we thank you for these people who awaken us to the needs of others and to the call to work for peace and justice in our world so that one day we will join hands before you, our God, and say,
"Free at last, free at last.
Great God Almighty, in your love, we are free at last!"

The Table Gathering

LEADER: Because the spirit of God lives in us, we each give vision and shape to the dream of one people living in justice and peace. We gather before our table of brotherhood and sisterhood on which we have placed who we are through what we dream.

(pause for gathering)

To the banquet table of the Lord we have all been invited. We recognize this call through a reading from the Book of Revelations.

READER 6: "I saw an angel standing on the sun and shouting in a loud voice, 'Come and gather together for God's great feast.' Then I heard the sound of a voice saying, 'Praise God all people both great and small. Let us rejoice and be glad, let us give praise for God's greatness. Happy are those who have been invited to the wedding feast.' Then I saw a new heaven and a new earth. And a loud voice spoke again: 'Now God's home is with all people. God lives with them and they are God's people. All tears have been wiped from their eyes. And there is no more death, no more grief or crying or pain. Come and gather together at the table for God's great feast.'"

Revelations 19:17, 5, 9, 21:1–4 (adapted)

LEADER: As we wait this day, we speak of who we are through the work we do and the dreams we share.

(Participants talk about and explain their placemats.)

As we yearn for this banquet day, as we work to make this old world into a new one, as we help one another live the dream, let us join hands and say together the prayer of the promised and dreamed-for kingdom of God.

ALL: Our Father who art in heaven, hallowed be your name; your kingdom come; your will be done on earth as it is in heaven. Give us this day our daily bread; and forgive us our trespasses as we forgive those who trespass against us; and lead us not into temptation, but deliver us from evil. Amen.

Valentine's Day

A Background Reflection

Valentine was a priest and bishop of early times. Legends surround his life and the custom of sending love letters on this day. Rather than sort out truth from fiction, we celebrate Valentine's memory and look each year at our call to be loving people. Valentine's Day reminds us to turn toward God in love and to live that love with one another.

Though the word *love* has become trite, its meaning lies in John's profound statement "not that we have loved God, but that [God] loved us" (1 John 4:10). As children, we are told of God's love for us and only slowly during our lives do we accept this overwhelming fact. Just as moments arise in our lives when we are willing to accept God's constant love for us, so also moments arise in which we discover that, because of God's love, we are loveable and capable of giving love.

Love is difficult, yet we are called to become lovers. Valentine's Day gives us the chance to look closely at the variety of ways we love. When we love, we choose the best for another. We communicate from our center to another's center. We make a commitment to be *with* and *for* another person. In love, we give our joy, our interests, our understanding; we give that which makes us most alive.

This is the deepest mystery of our faith: God is love. We learn of this love through God's sending of Jesus into the world. Jesus is the sign of God's love for us, and he tells us what he told his disciples:

> "I love you just as the Father loves me; remain in my love. If you obey my commands, you will remain in my love, just as I have obeyed my Father's commands and remain in his love."
>
> John 15: 9–10

Celebrating Valentine's Day helps children look at more than the getting and giving of valentines; it gives us all the chance to look at where love comes from. It helps us see that our ability to love comes from having been loved first — by our parents, family, and most of all by God. This prayer service should be a happy celebration, one in which the children feel good about being loved.

Preparation

directions

Complete the projects.

Select two readers.

Practice singing the song "Kum Ba Yah" with the following words: "Someone's giving, Lord . . . ," "Someone's thanking, Lord . . . ," "Someone's loving, Lord . . . ."

During the celebration, each participant will receive a small heart. After the celebration, encourage the participants to write messages of love on their hearts to give to loved ones.

Gather the participants around a table on which you have placed a bowl of treats and the flowerpot.

materials

red construction paper
a stick on which to mount a large
    construction-paper heart
a stapler or tape
a flowerpot filled with sand
a bowl of candy hearts, gumdrops, raisins,
    or other simple treats

Projects

Have the participants use the pattern below
to make a large red construction-paper heart.
(Optional: Paste a collage of magazine
pictures showing love on the heart.) Staple
or tape the heart to a stick and stand it in a
flowerpot filled with sand.

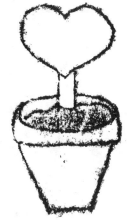

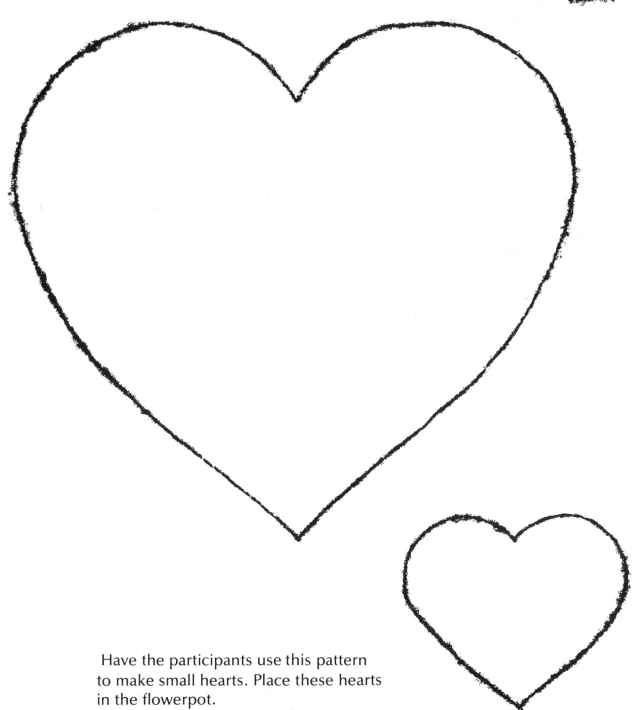

Have the participants use this pattern
to make small hearts. Place these hearts
in the flowerpot.

15

Prayer Celebration

Introduction

LEADER: Today we're here to celebrate the love that is in our lives. Valentine reminds us to take time out to think about how wonderful it is to be loved and to love others. We gather around the heart, a sign of our love for one another. Let us now enjoy this celebration of love.

First Reading

LEADER: The Bible tells us many things about love.

READER 1: Dear Friends, let us love one another, because love comes from God. Everyone who loves is a child of God and knows God. The person who does not love does not know God, for God is love. God showed love for us by sending Jesus into the world, so that we might have life through him. This then is what love is: Love is not that we have loved God, but that God has loved us and has sent Jesus so that our sins are forgiven.

(adapted from 1 John 4:7–10)

LEADER: Thank you, God, for loving us.

ALL: Thank you, God, for loving us.

LEADER: Thank you, God, for sending your Son.

ALL: Thank you, God, for sending your Son.

LEADER: Thank you, Jesus, for showing us how to love.

ALL: Thank you, Jesus, for showing us how to love.

Second Reading

READER 2: And now I give you a new commandment: Love one another as I have loved you. If you love one another, then people will know that you are my followers.

(adapted from John 13:34-35)

LEADER: Let us think and pray about the meaning of this reading in our own lives. Sometimes it is hard to wish the best for someone else.

Help us, O Lord, to be glad for others' successes. (Pause.)

Help us to have an open heart and love as Jesus loved. (Pause.)

When we show that we care for others, people can recognize a little of Jesus in us. Help us, O Lord, to care for others even when we don't feel like it. (Pause.)

(Optional: If you made a love collage on the large heart, spend time now sharing why you chose particular pictures. The leader first shares his or her reasons for choosing a picture. Then each person in the group follows.)

Presentation of Hearts

LEADER: Each of us is loved and capable of loving others. Both are God's gifts. As I call your name, please come forward and receive a heart, a sign of God's love for us, a sign of our willingness to love others as Jesus did.

(Calls each participant by name, saying:)

<u>(Name)</u>, receive this heart. Go and love as Jesus loved.

Litany of Love

LEADER: Love is patient; love is kind.

ALL: Love is patient; love is kind.

LEADER: Love enjoys others for themselves.

ALL: Love enjoys others for themselves.

LEADER: Love is generous and courteous, easy to be with.

ALL: Love is generous and courteous, easy to be with.

LEADER: Love forgives and forgets others' wrongs.

ALL: Love forgives and forgets others' wrongs.

LEADER: Love lasts a long time.

ALL: Love lasts a long time.

(adapted from 1 Corinthians 13:4-7)

LEADER: As part of this celebration, let us share food as another sign of loving and caring for each other.

ALL: (Share the treat.)

Closing Prayer

LEADER: With the Spirit, may we all go forth, as Valentine did, to love God, ourselves, and others.

Let us sing together:

ALL: Someone's giving, Lord, Kumbaya,
Someone's giving, Lord, Kumbaya,
Someone's giving, Lord, Kumbaya,
Oh Lord, Kumbaya.

Someone's thanking, Lord....

Someone's loving, Lord....

Mardi Gras / Ash Wednesday

A Background Reflection

There are rhythms to life—in the four seasons, in day and night, in the beating of our hearts, in breathing in and out. We live opposites daily through beginnings and endings, goodbyes and hellos, waitings and fulfillings. The yearning of the heart reflects itself in apparent contradictions—wanting to celebrate and to abstain, to rejoice and to mourn. Ecclesiastes captures this spirit rhythm in which we live by announcing that there is a "time for everything." The celebration of Mardi Gras and the immediate entry into Lent with Ash Wednesday offers us an experience of opposites—of celebrating and abstaining.

Carnival time, a time of feasting, revelery, and gaiety, which culminates on Mardi Gras day, actually begins on Twelfth Night (the twelfth night after Christmas). During the following weeks, parades and masked balls are held. When I was in New Orleans, it was the custom for young people to gather weekly for King Cake parties. A bean was baked into a specially made round cake with the carnival colors of purple, green, and gold. Whoever got the bean was king or queen for the evening and had the party at his or her home the following week. This continued until Mardi Gras.

On the Tuesday before Ash Wednesday, Mardi Gras day, people gather in the streets dressed in costume to watch parades of gaily and elaborately decorated floats from which people throw favors and trinkets. The best-known carnival celebrations are centered in New Orleans, the Caribbean Islands, Trinidad, Rio de Janeiro, and parts of France.

These carnival celebrations encourage a sense of make-believe, with people masking themselves and wearing costumes. For an entire day, one can pretend to be someone else, can play a role. Like the child or the actor, we are invited to play "let's pretend." Actually, in earlier times people wore these masks to scare away the demons who were thought to spread the darkness of winter.

The French name Mardi Gras means Fat Tuesday. It was the custom on this day to eat as much fat as possible before the rigid abstinence from all these foods during the forty days of Lent. Pancakes were eaten in England, while in France and Germany, doughnuts fried in deep fat were the ritual food. Even the leader of Mardi Gras parades who rides a float with a huge ox, and the gaily costumed butchers who throw sweets and trinkets, are there to remind us of what we are soon to be without.

On Ash Wednesday morning, the debris of Mardi Gras lies in the streets, in sharp contrast to the people who are walking home from church with a smear of ashes (from the burning of previous year's blessed palms) on their foreheads as they begin the journey of Lent. For all Christian churches, Lent is a forty-day period of preparation that ends in Holy Week and builds to the joyous celebration of Easter. This is a time of increased penance, prayer, service to others, and almsgiving. It is the traditional time to pay increased attention to God in your life.

Sprinkling your head with ashes is an ancient sign of repentence we have accepted from Jewish tradition. Jonah (3:5–9), Jeremiah (6:26, 25:3), and Matthew (11:21) all show that wearing ashes was a sign of penance and sorrow. The Christian custom of marking the head with ashes began during the papacy of Gregory the Great (6th century A.D.), when public penitents came barefoot to the church to perform penances for wrongdoing. In recognition that no one is free from sin and wanting to stand by these penitents, friends and relatives began to come. Soon ashes were given to the entire gathered assembly. Many Christian denominations today observe Ash Wednesday with the distribution of ashes.

Preparations

directions

Choose three areas for each of the three stations.

At the first station, gather with noisemakers and masks.

At the second station hang streamers.

At the third station hang the blue panel with a cross for the season of winter and place before it a purple-covered box or chest (to use for burying the streamers during the ceremony).

Also place here pencils and papers and a container for burning, such as a metal plate or pan.

Make masks.

Make streamers.

Choose two readers.

Gather noisemakers (a drum, a hand bell, tambourines, and so forth). These will be used at Station One, for one of the litany prayers, and to mark the transition from Mardi Gras to Ash Wednesday.

Be prepared to call each participant by name — write a list, or provide name tags.

Explain to participants that during the ceremony they will be writing on small pieces of paper, which will then be burned. Explain the significance of burning one's Lenten promise. (Like smoke, our spirits lift in knowing we can do all things in Jesus.)

Teach participants the version of "When the Saints Go Marching In" used in the service.

Choose appropriate music if you wish to use it during the distribution of the ashes from the burned Lenten promises.

materials

Winter panel (blue)
Small scraps of paper
Pencils
Metal plate for burning
Noisemakers
Purple, gold, green crepe paper
Scissors and crayons
Box
Purple cloth or paper

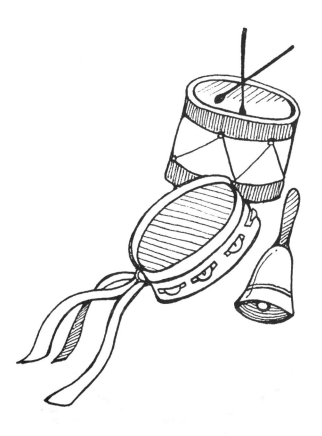

Project

Make long streamers from the crepe paper (the carnival colors are purple, gold, and green). Cut 1-inch × 6-foot strips. With felt-tip markers or white paper, write or cut out letters or words expressing the carnival season, such as Joy, Happy, Hope, Wow, Alleluia. (Make sure that Alleluia is included.) Place words on streamers.

Make masks.

With purple cloth or paper, make a large cross, and pin it to the winter panel.

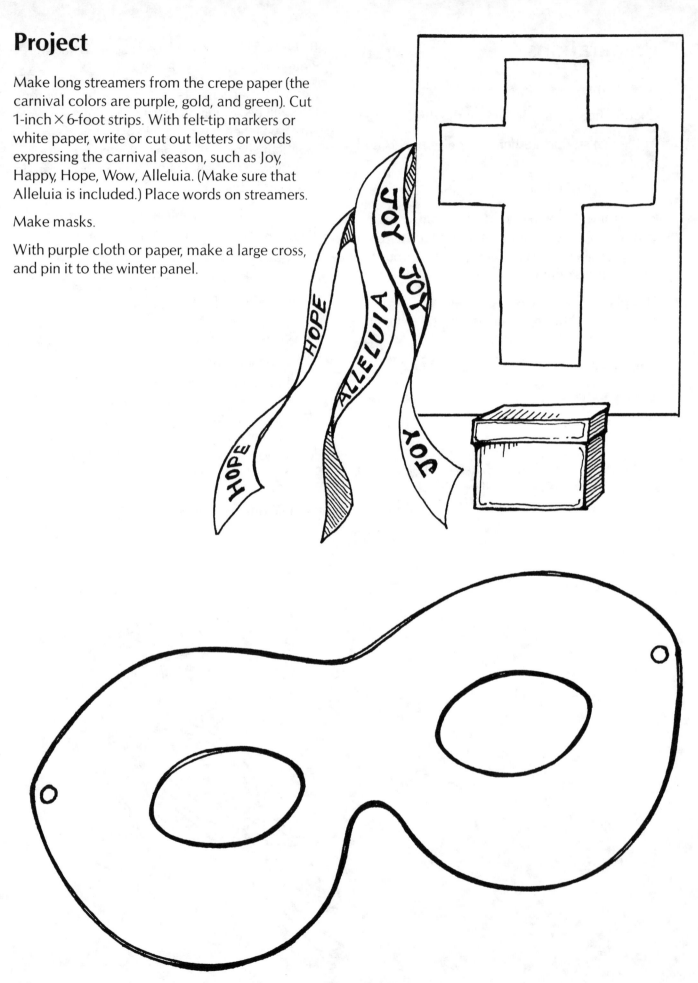

Prayer Celebration

Opening Greeting

LEADER: It is said that there is a time for everything, a time to celebrate and to abstain, a time to rejoice and to mourn. We come together to mark the days of opposites, Mardi Gras and Ash Wednesday.

At First Station

LEADER: In the spirit of the Carnival season, we gather with music, song, movement, and hearts of joy to celebrate Mardi Gras. We wear masks and enter into a world of make-believe and pretend.

(Masks are put on.)

With our noisemakers we tell the world of our joy in being able to celebrate life.

(noisemakers)

And through movement and song we sing,
(to the tune of "When the Saints Go Marching In")
O, when the sun begins to shine
O, when the sun begins to shine
O, Lord, I want to be in that number
When the sun begins to shine

When our hearts show out their love,

(Sing while marching around.)

At Second Station

LEADER: We gather before our carnival streamers, which tell of our joy before the Lord as we speak our praise, our Alleluia.

READER 1: Lord, from where we have come and to where we are going, we say, "Amen. Praise God. Alleluia."

ALL: Amen. Praise God. Alleluia.

(Music makers play during response.)

READER 1: For beginnings, middles, and ends and all the moments of being alive, we say, "Amen, Praise God, Alleluia."

ALL: Amen. Praise God. Alleluia.

(Music makers play.)

READER 1: For faith to believe in mystery, we say, "Amen, Praise God. Alleluia."

ALL: Amen. Praise God. Alleluia.

(Music makers play.)

READER 1: For hope that opens us to surprise, we say, "Amen. Praise God. Alleluia."

(Music makers play.)

For love that gives us grateful hearts, we say, "Amen, Praise God. Alleluia."

ALL: Amen. Praise God. Alleluia.

(Music makers play.)

READER 1: Through God and with God, in the unity of the spirit, all honor and glory is yours, world without end.

ALL: Amen.

(Bell or drum slowly intones to count of twelve as everyone becomes silent and takes off masks. As they move to Third Station, they take pencil and paper from box.)

At Third Station

LEADER: We begin the season of Lent as we stand before the cross, a sign of our forty-day journey toward Easter. This is our time to pay attention to God in our life through prayer, penance, and doing acts of loving-kindness to others.

Write on your paper one thing that you promise to do this Lent to become more aware of God in yourself and others.

(pause)

As I call you by name, come forward and place your folded paper in the plate in front of the cross.

(calling of names)

We gather these offerings and light them. As we watch them burn, we deepen our promises in our heart. As the smoke lifts, so do our spirits in knowing that we can do all things in Jesus who lives in us and among us.

(lighting and burning)

A Reading

LEADER: In this reading from Joel, we reflect on the call to turn to God with all our heart for God is tender and compassionate.

READER 2: "Yet even now, says the Lord, return to me with all your heart, with fasting, with weeping, and with mourning; and rend your hearts and not your garments. Return to the Lord, your God, for God is gracious and merciful, slow to anger, and abounding in steadfast love."

Joel 2:12–13

This is the Word of the Lord.

ALL: Thanks be to God.

LEADER: Now take a moment to think of the ways you can turn to God with all your heart.

Blessing and Giving of Ashes

LEADER: We extend our hands over the ashes in blessing. Lord, Bless these ashes, which we use as a sign that we have turned to you with all our heart. Pardon our wrongdoings. Keep us faithful to our Lenten promises.

(Leader marks the forehead of each person with the ashes while saying:)

"Keep Lent and turn to God with all your heart."

The Alleluia Farewell

LEADER: Our days are now different. The Alleluia, our acclamation of cheer, will not be spoken or sung during Lent.

In ceremony, we take down our streamers and place them in our Lenten box.

(pause)

On Easter, we will lift them from this darkened place, and in the new light of the resurrection display and proclaim the Alleluia of our Risen Lord.

Let us bow our heads for God's blessing.

Come back to the Lord with all your heart.

ALL: Amen.

LEADER: Leave the past in ashes.

ALL: Amen.

LEADER: Turn to God with prayers and fasting.

ALL: Amen.

LEADER: For God is tender and compassionate.

ALL: Amen.

LEADER: In silence and quiet, let us go forth to love and serve the Lord through the way we live our Lenten promises.

ALL: In the name of the Father, and of the Son, and of the Holy Spirit, Amen.

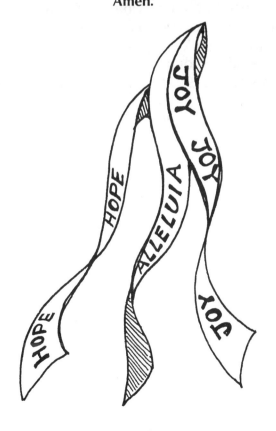

Lent

A Background Reflection

Ash Wednesday begins the forty days of preparation for celebrating the resurrection. This period we call Lent means spring, and we celebrate it in memory of the forty days Jesus spent alone praying in the desert.

Lent is a time for strengthening our faith, a time to reflect on who we are and where we are going. It is a time of quietness and prayer, a time of penance and meditation, a time to become aware of our strength and weakness.

Just as Jesus spent forty days in preparation for his work of redemption, so we, too, prepare for our own redemption. During Lent, we enter into Jesus' redemption by choosing to look at ourselves, at how we talk and listen, how we think and act, how we are with others. Lent provides many opportunities for people to choose to do renewing activities, such as visiting someone who is lonely, giving up something like television, spending a certain amount of time in prayer, choosing to fast, attending church services.

Ash Wednesday is a good day to choose what you, your class, or your family will do to prepare for the new life of the resurrection. Review and renew these resolutions periodically during Lent.

On Shrove Tuesday, the day before Ash Wednesday, some families have a Mardi Gras celebration and make gaily-colored paper or cloth banners of praise with words on them such as *alleluia, new life, joy*. In ceremony, they bury these banners the following day and resurrect them on Easter morning in a joyful celebration of the risen Lord.

Lent urges us to identify and walk with Jesus as he travels toward Jerusalem and the place of his death and resurrection. In a spirit of renewal and conversion we observe Lent by reflecting on the central events of Jesus' life and welcoming this opportunity to grow through forgiving and being forgiven.

Preparation

directions

Complete the projects.

Choose a leader and three readers.

Choose three participants to carry the lighted candle, the Bible, and the basket of small crosses.

(Sing an appropriate closing song.)

During the celebration, each participant will receive a small cross. After the celebration, encourage the participants to hang the crosses in their rooms during Lent and to decorate them for Easter.

Gather the participants in a semicircle before the large cross.

materials

small twigs, two for each participant
two large branches
string
a basket
a Bible
a candle

Projects

Use string to tie two branches together to
make a large cross. Stand the cross up
against a wall for the celebration.

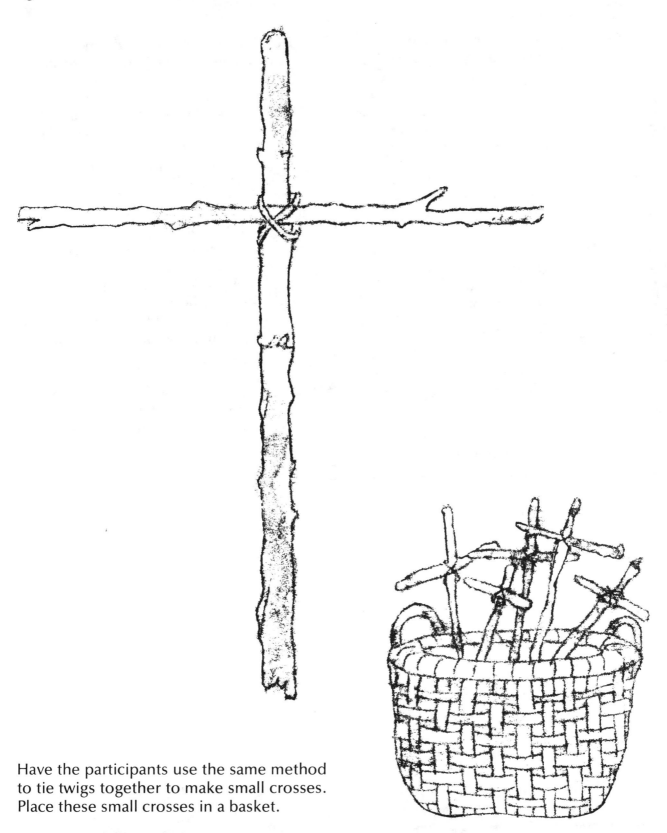

Have the participants use the same method
to tie twigs together to make small crosses.
Place these small crosses in a basket.

Prayer Celebration

Introduction

LEADER: For forty days we prepare for the new life of Easter. The cross reminds us that we all have hard things to do in life. When we accept these things as Jesus accepted his cross, we know we are following Jesus.

ALL: In the name of the Father, and of the Son, and of the Holy Spirit.

LEADER: We bring a lighted candle as a sign that Jesus is with us as we face hard things and take up our cross to follow him.

(One participant places the candle before the cross.)

We bring a Bible. In reading the Word of God we begin to know and understand his way.

(One participant places the Bible before the cross.)

We bring a Bible. In reading the Word of God we begin to know and understand the ways of God.

(One participant places the basket of crosses before the large cross.)

Let us think about accepting hardship into our lives — not for its own sake, but in order to grow in a more loving relationship with God and with others.

First Reading

READER 1: Jesus took Peter and James and John with him into a garden and asked them to wait with him while he prayed. When Jesus finished praying, he went back and found them asleep. He said to Peter, "Are you sleeping? Could you not watch one hour with me?"

(adapted from Mark 14:33, 37)

Taking time to pray can be a reminder to us to use God's name carefully and respectfully. Think of times during the day when we might stop and give thanks for all that God does for us.

(Pause for reflection.)

ALL: We adore you and we bless you, Lord, because by your holy cross you have redeemed the world.

Second Reading

READER 2: They asked a man who was coming in from the country to carry the cross. His name was Simon of Cyrene.

(adapted from Mark 15:21)

LEADER: Think of ways in which we are like Simon. Do we help others? Do we try to understand persons who are outside of our usual circle of friends?

(Pause for reflection.)

ALL: We adore you and we bless you, Lord, because by your holy cross you have redeemed the world.

Third Reading

READER 3:   Jesus said, "Whoever wishes to be my follower must think of other people first and must take up the cross daily and follow me. Whoever would save his life will lose it, and whoever loses his life for my sake will save it."

(adapted from Luke 9:23)

Let us think about how we do our work. Is it easy to give up when the work gets hard? Do we accept and love the person that each of us is, knowing that God made each of us to be ourself alone?

(Pause for reflection.)

ALL: We adore you and we bless you, Lord, because by your holy cross you have redeemed the world.

Calling of Names

LEADER: As your name is called, please come forward.

(Repeats the following ceremony for each participant.)

<u>(Name)</u>_____, are you willing to be open to new experiences, even hard ones, and to take up your cross and follow Jesus?

PERSON: I am.

LEADER: Receive this cross as a sign of your promise.

(Gives a small cross to the participant.)

Closing Prayer

LEADER: Lord, we are all here with our weaknesses and strengths as we take up our crosses and follow you. We are not afraid of suffering or hardships when we know you are with us, Lord, and when we know we have one another's support.

(Sing an appropriate closing song.)

Holy (Maundy) Thursday

A Background Reflection

The Thursday of Holy Week recalls the Last Supper that Jesus shared with his disciples on the night before he died. On that evening Jesus celebrated the Passover in an upper room of a Jewish friend's home.

On the night the Jews escaped from slavery in Egypt, they observed the first Passover by sacrificing a lamb and sprinkling its blood on their doorways so that *the Lord will pass over that door and not let the destroyer come into that house* (adapted from Exodus 12:23). Since they departed so hastily from Egypt, there was no time for the bread to rise. In remembrance, Jews eat only unleavened bread, or matzah, during Passover.

The main Passover celebration is called a Seder. Literally, Seder means "order," referring to the order of the ceremony set up in ancient ritual books. Certain things are important to the Seder: special foods, the reading of the Haggadah, (the story of the celebration), and the questioning by the youngest child as to the meaning of the Seder. In most Jewish communities, families repeat Seder on the second night of the eight-day feast of Passover.

When Jesus celebrated Passover at the Last Supper, he used the occasion to offer himself as a gift to his apostles. *When he broke bread, he said, "This is my Body"; when he took the wine, he said, "This is my Blood." Jesus then asked his friends to "do this in memory of me"* (adapted from Luke 22:19–20). We continue to celebrate the Lord's Supper in memory of Jesus. After the supper, Jesus discussed the meaning of the kingdom and washed the feet of his friends as a call to his followers to serve others as he did.

Many families observe the Passover meal, linking it to the Lord's Supper.

Together they remember that

> This means that every time you eat this bread and drink from this cup you proclaim the Lord's death until he comes.
>
> 1 Corinthians 11:26

Preparation

directions

This shortened, adapted Passover Seder should be celebrated within the context of a meal at which lamb is served. If this is not possible, have a symbolic lamb on your Seder table.

Complete the project.

Choose a leader (the father) and two readers (the mother and the youngest child).

Choose and practice an appropriate song to sing at the end of the celebration.

Set the table. Each participant should have a cup and a plate on which you have placed a green vegetable (parsley or celery), a bitter herb (radish or horseradish), and a small amount of salt.

In the center of the table place candles, one large cup, a large matzah, and a bowl of horoses (a mixture of sliced apples, chopped nuts, and cinnamon).

Place a bowl of water, a cloth, wine or grape juice and a plate of matzah near the leader's place.

materials

burlap or posterboard
felt or construction paper
scissors
crayons and/or felt-tipped pens
paste or glue
a yardstick
stapler or tape
string
food and utensils for the meal (see
    directions above)
candles

Project

Have the participants make symbols of the Lord's Supper and paste or glue them on burlap or posterboard. Staple or tape this banner to a yardstick. Attach string to both ends of the yardstick so that you can hang the banner near your celebration table.

Prayer Celebration

Introduction

LEADER: Today we remember that Jesus and his friends celebrated a Jewish Passover, a Seder, a solemn meal carried out according to ancient Jewish ritual. Let us pretend we are in the upper room of a house. We are celebrating the passover of God's people from slavery to freedom.

Lighting the Festival Lights

LEADER:
(FATHER) We, (name of family or group), light candles to remind ourselves that Jesus, the light of the world, is coming.

READER:
(MOTHER) (Lights the candles and says:) Blessed are you, God, King of the Universe, who has commanded us to light the festival lights. Blessed are you, God, for you have made us alive and keep us alive through all seasons. During this spring season may our home be filled with peace and joy.

READER: Food is always blessed before it is eaten. A long time ago, the Jews blessed their bread and wine at their Jewish Passover. Just as they did, we bless ours tonight (today). The presider at the Lord's Supper also blesses the food at the offertory.

All: Thank you, God, for choosing us to be your people. We celebrate all you have given us.

The Elijah Cup

LEADER: (Opens the front door.)

READER: There is an extra cup on this table. We would give this cup of honor to any stranger who should come and ask to keep the Passover with us. We call this cup the Elijah cup because Elijah is known to have helped the poor. We have opened the door to welcome anyone who may stand outside. We pray for the hungry and the poor and wish they could celebrate this Passover meal with us.

Pouring and Drinking the Wine

LEADER: Four times during the Seder meal, wine is passed. We will pass the wine only twice. Usually the wine is poured from one bowl to show oneness.

(The leader pours wine or grape juice into each person's cup.)

At the Last Supper, Christ poured wine for his friends and said, "Take this and drink it. I tell you that I will not drink of the fruit of the vine again until I drink it with you in my Father's Kingdom."

ALL: Blessed are you, God, for making this fruit of the vine.

(The participants drink their wine.)

Washing of Hands

LEADER: We must clean not only our hands but also our hearts and minds. The presider washes his hands just as Christ washed the feet of his friends at the Last Supper. This gesture shows how much he loves us; it calls us to serve others.

(The leader washes his or her hands and then washes the hands of all the participants as a sign of willingness to serve.)

ALL: Thank you, God, King of the universe, for showing us how to serve others.

Eating of Greens

LEADER: We eat these greens as a symbol that nature comes to life in spring-time. Following the Jewish custom, we dip the greens in salt and pray:

ALL: Blessed are you, God, King of the universe, creator of the fruit of the earth.

(Participants dip the greens in salt and eat them.)

Questions

LEADER: Now we will retell the story of the first passover. God told us to do this in the book of Exodus. The first part of Mass and of our meal today instructs us. The youngest person present asks the four traditional questions.

YOUNGEST: Why is this night different from all other nights? Why on this night do we eat bitter herbs? Why do we hold this meal on this night?

LEADER: (Reads Exodus 12 or an adapted version of the story.)

Meaning of the Food

LEADER: To show that the food for this celebration is a symbol of God helping the people escape from Egypt, we will lift the food and explain its meaning. This is part of the Seder meal for Jewish people.

ALL: What is matzah?

LEADER: Matzah is unleavened bread, bread made without yeast. Yeast makes bread rise, but it takes time. Because the Israelites had to make hasty preparations to leave Egypt, they did not have time to wait for the bread to rise.

ALL: What is the meaning of moror?

LEADER: Moror means bitter herbs. We eat these herbs to remind us that the lives of God's people were made bitter by slavery in Egypt.

(The participants eat the bitter herbs.)

ALL: What is the meaning of horoses?

LEADER: Horoses is a mixture of apples, nuts and cinnamon. The horoses looks like the mortar which the people of Israel used to build the Pharaoh's cities.

(Each participant breaks a piece of matzah, places horoses on it, and eats.)

ALL: What is the meaning of pesach?

LEADER: Pesach means paschal lamb. We offer this gift to the Lord in memory of that night when God helped our forefathers in Egypt. The blood of the lamb was placed on the door and the angel of death passed over that house. That night the people passed over into the land of liberty and freedom.

LEADER: Just as we shared wine from one bowl, we break one piece of bread and pass it to everyone, signifying unity. Long ago the householder gave a piece of bread to show love. This gives special meaning to the act of Christ in taking a piece of bread and handing it to Judas. That gesture was a last loving appeal to Judas. But as the Gospel tells us "he, having received the morsel, went out immediately."

(Each participant takes a piece of matzah.)

ALL: Blessed are you, Lord God, King of the universe, who has made us hold your commandments and has told us to eat this unleavened bread.

(Everyone eats the matzah.)

The Meal

(If you are having a full meal, retell the story of the Last Supper during the eating of the meal. If not, proceed to the final blessing.)

Final Blessing

LEADER: It is the custom to end the Passover meal with this piece of unleavened bread.

(The leader breaks the matzah in the center of the table and passes it to all.)

It was probably at this moment that Christ took bread, broke it and gave it to his friends saying, "Take and eat, this is my body which is to be given for you."

(All eat a piece of the matzah.)

The cup of wine was passed.

(The leader pours wine or grape juice into each cup.)

After he had eaten, Christ took a cup and offered thanks and gave it to his friends and said, "This is the chalice, the New Testament in my blood which shall be shed for you."

(All drink the wine or grape juice.)

The Lord bless you and keep you. The Lord make his face shine upon you and have mercy on you. The Lord give you peace.

ALL: So be it. So be it. So be it.

(Sing closing song.)

Good Friday

A Background Reflection

The anniversary of the passion and death of Christ is commemorated on Friday of Holy Week —Good Friday. Since the life of Christ, Good Friday has been celebrated as a day of sadness, mourning, fasting, and prayer. For Catholics, Good Friday and Ash Wednesday are the only two remaining days when the church asks members to fast.

There are many different rituals for Good Friday. A three-hour devotion is popular in both Catholic and Protestant churches and consists of meditations on the seven last words Jesus spoke from the cross. Hymns are usually sung between these meditations.

The Adoration of the Cross is another Good Friday devotion. During the Adoration of the Cross, people kneel, bow, and prostrate themselves three times as they advance toward the cross. In Catholic churches today, the presider unveils the crucifix in three stages while singing, "This is the wood of the cross on which hung the Savior of the world." The people are then invited to come forth and kiss the feet of the image.

Besides the Adoration of the Cross, the Stations of the Cross are offered on Good Friday by many churches. It is said that during the Crusades Christians visiting Jerusalem marked off the sites where they thought the Christ's passion had occurred. On returning home, these travelers continued this devotion by erecting memorials of these stations inside their churches or outside in their fields. Today, many Catholic and Episcopal churches have carvings of these passion scenes on their walls.

St. Augustine said that from the moment of Christ's death to the morning of his resurrection was forty hours. From this forty-hour "wake" grew the Forty Hours devotion of fast and prayer that became popular at other chosen times of the year. This devotion is still honored in many churches today.

To commemorate Good Friday, many home observances among families have been faithfully followed. In England plain rice cooked in milk became the traditional Good Friday meal, while the Irish had their "black fast" of only water or tea for the day. In central Europe, vegetable soup and bread were eaten standing and in silence. Today, many people fast, eating only rice during the day or soup at night. A mood of silence continues to permeate the day. Church altars are stripped bare; so are many kitchen tables, left with only a cactus plant as a centerpiece.

The custom of making and eating hot cross buns on Good Friday dates back to pagan days, when tiny cakes were offered to the goddess known as the Queen of Heaven. Made of spiced dough, round in shape, with a cross of icing on top, hot cross buns to commemorate Easter became popular in Europe and later in America. The buns were considered blessed. If eaten on Good Friday, they protected you against sickness and dangers such as house fires and lightning. Some people would keep a hot cross bun throughout the year in their home and eat it as medicine or wear as a charm. From the hot cross bun developed the widespread custom of marking a new loaf of bread with the sign of the cross before cutting it.

Actually, many popular observances once done in a spirit of true reverence later gave rise to superstitions. For example, it was said that craftspeople were not to swing hammers or drive nails on the day Christ was nailed to a cross, and people were not to use instruments made of iron. So carpenters, plumbers, and blacksmiths did not work on Good Friday. Vinegar, used to mock Jesus' thirst on the cross, was eliminated from the day's menus. Washing clothes on Good Friday, was supposed to bring bad luck for the year. In Spain developed the custom of dipping up water from wells or rivers before sunrise without speaking. This gesture was thought to have healing power and to ensure that the people's source of water would remain pure all year. From Central Europe came the ritual of planting parsley, beans, and peas for a good year's crop. Superstitions are not "true," but they do reflect people's need for tradition, symbolism, and ritual.

Today people also need some tangible things to do—or not to do—in giving focus to this day. For example, early Christians refused to greet anyone on Good Friday with *Shalom* ("peace be with you"), for this was what Judas said in betraying Jesus. They would only use the greeting "the Light of God be with you." So we look to find rituals to mark this day.

We mark the anniversary of the death of someone close to us through rituals—lighting a candle, celebrating the Eucharist, visiting the grave. And we share stories about that person—we remember again that person's presence in our lives. On Good Friday, too, we can remember how Jesus has touched our lives in the past and speak, through stories, of Jesus' continued presence in our lives.

Preparations

directions

Hang the green panel for the spring season. Make and display a cross of bare branches.

Choose readers for a boy with loaves and fishes, a woman in a crowd, the daughter of Jairus, Peter, Mary Magdalene, and Mary. Each has a sign to place before the cross.

Acquaint participants on how to bow, bending from waist, with reverence before the cross.

Have slips of paper and pencils, pens, or markers ready for Your Remembrance section. On their completion during ceremony, collect these slips in basket.

Place hot cross buns before the cross.

Choose appropriate instrumental music.

You may want to hold the branch cross for the closing blessing.

materials

Green panel
Bare branches
Twine
Paper
Pens, pencils, magic markers

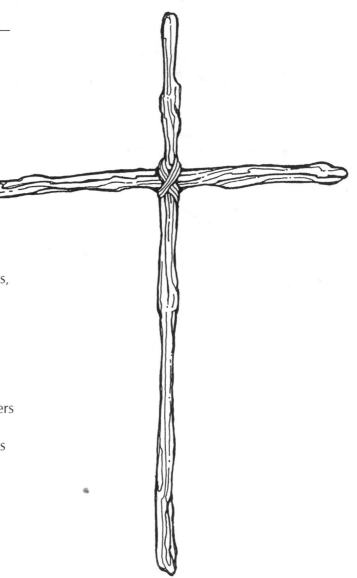

35

Project

With twine, make a cross from bare, found
branches. Make loaves and fishes, the word
help, a hand, fishing net, stones, a heart, for each
of the readers.

Make or buy hot cross buns.

Prayer Celebration

Opening Greeting

LEADER: This is a memorial to our Lord;
this is the anniversary of the
passion and death of Christ.
As we stand before this simple
cross, we remember what
Jesus did for us—
he died for us,
he rose,
and he will come again.
We bow before your cross
Lord, and say,
"We adore you, O Lord,"

ALL: We adore you, O Lord.

LEADER: "And we bless you"

ALL: And we bless you

LEADER: "Because by your holy cross"

ALL: Because by your holy cross

LEADER: "You have redeemed the
world."

ALL: You have redeemed the world.

Francis of Assisi

In Remembrance

LEADER: We speak from our hearts of
the way Jesus has touched our
life. These words are spoken in
remembrance of Jesus by
people who knew him. Their
words become our tribute to
Jesus.

LITTLE BOY WITH LOAVES AND FISHES: "People sometimes say that
when you are little you cannot
do much. But this is not
always true. It does not matter
how old you are when you are
able to share. One day I was
hungry. My Mom had given
me lunch but I saved it while I
listened to Jesus talk. It started
getting late. I heard someone
asking if anyone had any food.
The people were hungry. Of
course I gave my bread and
fish. Wouldn't you? Jesus was
giving to the people by
comforting them and helping
them to love themselves
again. Even if it was not much,
I wanted to give something,
too. That is how I remember
Jesus—outside in an open
field—giving to the people."

LEADER: We thank the little boy with
the loaves and fishes for his
words of remembrance.
Before the cross, he bows and
places a sign of giving in his
life and in the life of Jesus.

(pause as boy does so)

And someone else remembers
Jesus.

A WOMAN IN THE CROWD: "I saw people trying to touch
him. He even had to go out in
a boat, for the crowds were so
great. I don't know why I was
there, just a face in the crowd,
but these people were there
because they believed in him.
Many were cured—deaf to
hear, blind to see, lame to
walk, those in sadness were
joyful again, those in doubt

now believed. I did not know why I had followed the crowd, why I was there. But suddenly I knew that I wanted to be free, I wanted to ask for help. And I did. And I was helped. That's how I remember Jesus — helping others and helping me."

LEADER: We thank a face in the crowd for her words of remembrance. Before the cross she bows and places a sign of helping in her life and in the life of Jesus.

(pause as woman does so)

And someone else remembers Jesus.

DAUGHTER OF JAIRUS: "Once I was so sick my father went looking for Jesus to see if he could help me. My father was an important man in our village. But when he found Jesus he fell on his knees and begged him to come to me. My father loved me very much; so did Jesus, for he came right away. They tell me he stretched out his hand over me, and said some words of blessing. I remember opening my eyes and looking at his face — it was so kind and compassionate. He told the people to feed me and to take care of me. That is how I remember Jesus — caring for me and asking others to show that same care.

LEADER: We thank the little daughter of Jairus for her words of remembrance. Before the cross, she bows and places a

sign of caring in her life and in the life of Jesus.

(pause as daughter does so)

And someone else remembers Jesus.

PETER: "What can I say? I began to sink in the water because I did not believe. After hesitating with Jesus's request to throw the net over again after we have been fishing all night and had caught nothing, I fell on my knees when the net was full. I said I would never deny Jesus and I did — three times. And through all my doubts, he never stopped loving me and never stopped asking me to love others. He believed in me more than I believed in myself. That is how I remember Jesus — believing in me and accepting me in my strengths and weaknesses."

LEADER: We thank Peter for his words of remembrance. Before the cross, he bows and places a sign of believing in his life and in the life of Jesus.

(pause as Peter does so)

And someone else remembers Jesus.

MARY MAGDALENE: "I have known joy in my life, and sadness, too. Even when I had done many wrong things and people wanted to stone me, Jesus rescued me. He forgave me, too. I was never the same again. I became his faithful friend — helped him as best I could as he did the work of God. I knew he had to die. But I just could not believe it. The memory of that Friday is still deep within me. I do not know how I was ever able to stand there at the foot of the cross. I cried. That is how I remember Jesus—loving and forgiving others, even his enemies, before he died."

LEADER: We thank Mary Magdalene for her words of remembrance. Before the cross she bows and places a sign of forgiveness in her life and in the life of Jesus.

(pause as the Magdalene does so)

And someone else remembers Jesus.

MARY: "I held him as a baby in my arms—helped him to learn how to walk. And all during those thirty years, before he even began his ministry, I wondered what would happen to this son of mine. His compassion for people was so beautiful. I was there at Cana when he changed water to wine. I was there when he healed and comforted the people. I was there in Jerusalem for the Passover. And I was there when he died on the cross. And when they took him down from the cross, I held him in my arms, just like I once did when he was a baby. My son. What love you have for others. That is how I remember Jesus—as a mother remembers her son."

LEADER: We thank Mary for her words of remembrance. Before the cross she bows and places a sign of love in her life and in the life of Jesus.

(pause as Mary does so)

Your Remembrance

LEADER: What is your remembrance of Jesus?

(pause)

How would you speak of Jesus?

(pause)

How do you need Jesus in your life right now?

(pause)

On your paper, draw or write a sign or words for the way you remember Jesus.

(Music plays as these signs are made and collected by passed baskets.)

The Cross

LEADER: "Jesus was led away, and carrying his cross by himself set out to what is called Golgotha." (John 19:17). The cross is a sign of Jesus's love for us, a sign of his willingness to forgive us forever. Let Jesus carry your needs, carry your wrongdoings, carry your faults and weaknesses. That is why Jesus carried his cross—for you. That is why Jesus died—for you. Think of one wrongdoing, one weakness in which you are in need of forgiveness.

(pause)

In procession, let each of us go forth, bow before the cross, and as we touch the cross mentally place our wrongdoing on the cross.

(pause)

Jesus carried our sins, but he does not carry the memory of them. Forgiven, we are free to live for others and so we bow and say, "We adore you, O Lord, and we bless you,"

ALL: We adore you, O Lord, and we bless you,

LEADER: "Because by your cross you have redeemed the world.

ALL: Because by your cross you have redeemed the world.

A Psalm

LEADER: In gratitude and thanksgiving, and in the memory of Jesus, we pray his prayer to his father. Our response will be, "Father, I put my life in your hands."

ALL: Father, I put my life in your hands.

LEADER: In you, O Lord, I find protection
Rescue me when I am afraid.
Redeem me when I am ashamed.
In your hands, O Lord, I place my spirit.

ALL: Father, I put my life in your hands.

LEADER: Sometimes people make fun of me.
They laugh and turn their backs on me.
Sometimes I feel like a dish that is broken
for I am forgotten and not important to anyone.

ALL: Father, I put my life in your hands.

LEADER: I trust you, my Lord.
In faith I say, "You are my God."
Rescue me from people who want to hurt me.
In your hands hold me and love me.

ALL: Father, I put my life in your hands.

LEADER: Let your face shine bright upon me.
May your kindness and gentleness save me.
Give me courage and make me fearless.
In your hands, O Lord, I place my hope.

ALL: Father, I put my life in your hands."

Psalm 31 (adapted)

Closing Blessing

LEADER: As for the people of long ago, our hot cross buns remind us that we are bound to one another through the cross of Jesus. We break and pass one of our hot cross buns.

(pause

As we eat this bread, we pledge our willingness to help carry the burdens of others as Jesus carries us. Bow your head for God's blessing. Through the cross you brought joy to the world.

ALL: Amen.

LEADER: Through the cross we remember the way you gave your life to us.

ALL: Amen.

LEADER: Through the cross you carry our burdens.

ALL: Amen.

LEADER: In the name of God the creator,
the Son the redeemer,
and the Holy Spirit the life giver,
we go forth to carry the burdens of others.

ALL: Amen.

(Share and eat the hot cross buns.)

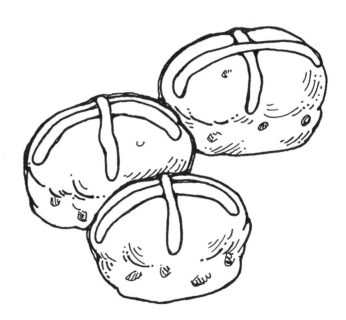

Easter

A Background Reflection

> You must not be afraid . . . I know you
> are looking for Jesus, who was
> crucified. He is not here; he has been
> raised, just as he said.
>
> Matthew 28:5–6

Easter is the greatest celebration of the
Christian Church. What Sunday is to the
week, Easter Sunday is to the liturgical
year. *This is the day the Lord has made. Let
us be happy, let us celebrate!* (adapted
from Psalm 118:24). The resurrection is the
reason for our faith, hope, and courage.
Through the resurrection of Jesus, we
know that one day we, too, will rise, body
and spirit, from the dead.

Members of the Council of Nicaea in
325 A.D. placed Easter on the first Sunday
following the first full moon after March
21. This date allowed pilgrims to have
moonlight for traveling to the great Easter
festivals of that day.

At Easter we celebrate the new life
given us in Jesus' death and resurrection
and recall that:

> By our baptism, then, we were buried
> with him and shared his death, in
> order that, just as Christ was raised
> from death by the glorious power of
> the Father, so also we might live a new
> life.
>
> Romans 6:4

At Easter we can remember and
celebrate our own baptism, the time we
chose new life. There are signs of new life
that we have experienced throughout the
different growing moments of daily living.

Children will enjoy making baptismal
stoles, placing on them signs of their
growth moments and wearing them for the
Easter church service. Family members can
wear them at a home celebration as
reminders of the new life received through
baptism. Wearing something new is a sign
that we are now living the new risen life of
Christ. Wearing new clothes to church is a
way of celebrating the meaning of Easter,
too.

Other activities for celebrating Easter
are: making a Christ candle to be used
throughout the year, placing fresh flowers
around the home, making Easter bread, or
decorating a resurrection cross. Children
enjoy dyeing and decorating Easter eggs.
The blessing of these eggs through a
church ritual helps children associate the
Easter egg with Christ's resurrection.

We ask you, Lord, to bless these eggs, to
make them a wholesome food for all of us
who gratefully have them in honor of the
resurrection of our Lord, Jesus Christ.

Preparation

directions

Complete the projects.

Choose a leader and one reader.

Practice singing an "Amen."

Choose participants to ring bells or play
tambourines during the prayer, Glory to
God.

Practice singing the following words to the
tune of "Michael, Row the Boat Ashore":

> Christ has risen as he said, Alleluia,
> Christ has risen as he said, Alleluia.
>
> We will rise again one day, Alleluia,
> We will rise again one day, Alleluia.

Decorate the area for the celebration with
the Easter pennants. Place fresh flowers,
the Christ candle, and candles
representing the participants on a table
and gather the participants around it.

materials

a Christ candle or the materials for making a Christ candle (see projects)
construction paper in assorted colors
scissors
crayons and/or felt-tipped pens
white cloth
felt or pieces of cloth in assorted colors
paste
bells and/or tambourines
small candles, one for each participant

Projects

Decorate a Christ candle. Use a heated blade to carve a cross, the first and last letters of the Greek alphabet, and this year's date on a large white candle, as shown. Mix tempera paint and egg yolk and use this mixture to color the carved areas. Place five cloves on the candle, as shown. (Light this candle during prayer times from Easter until the celebration of the Ascension.)

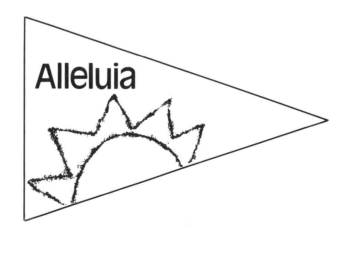

Have the participants make Easter pennants to decorate the prayer-celebration area.

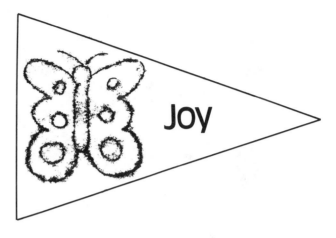

Have each participant make his or her own baptismal stole by making and attaching to an oblong piece of white cloth signs of new life experienced in growth moments.
Some examples:

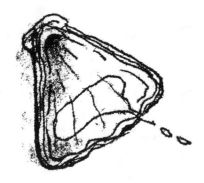

Baptism

Forgiving Someone

Family Reunion

Birthday

Getting a Driver's License

First Day of School

Prayer Celebration

Opening Prayer

LEADER: This is a most holy day, a day to rejoice, for our Lord Jesus Christ has risen from the dead.

ALL: Alleluia. Alleluia. Alleluia.

Blessing the Christ Candle

LEADER: Christ is the light of the world. Christ yesterday and today,

(Points to the cross and the date.)

The beginning and the end, Alpha and Omega,

(Points to the Greek letters.)

All time belongs to him and all the ages. To him be glory and power through every age forever.

ALL: Amen.

LEADER: By his holy wounds,

(Points to the cloves.)

May Christ our Lord guard and keep us.

ALL: Amen.

LEADER: May the light of Christ, rising in glory,

(Lights the candle.)

Dispel the darkness of our hearts and minds.

ALL: Amen.

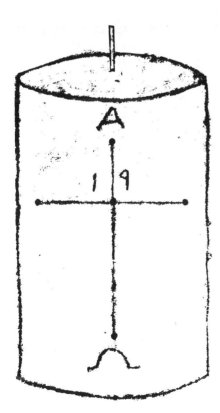

A Reading from the Gospel of Matthew

LEADER: You are the light of the world. A city built on the side of a mountain can be seen from far and near. People do not light lamps and then hide them under baskets. They set them out so that their light can be seen by all in the house. So must your light shine out to all people so that they may see goodness in your actions and give praise to God.

(adapted from Matthew 5:14-16)

LEADER: We are the light of the world and must live as children of the light.

(Lights the candles representing each of the participants, one at a time, saying:)

(Name)_____, receive the light of Christ.

Renewal of Faith

LEADER: Do you believe in God, the Father Almighty, creator of heaven and earth?

ALL: We do believe.

LEADER: Do you believe in Jesus Christ, his only Son, our Lord, who was born of the virgin, was crucified, died, and was buried, rose from the dead, and is now seated at the right hand of the Father?

ALL: We do believe.

LEADER: Do you believe in the Holy Spirit, the holy catholic church, the communion of saints, the forgiveness of sins, the resurrection of the body, and life everlasting?

ALL: We do believe.

LEADER: This is our faith. This is the faith of the church. We are proud to profess it, in Christ Jesus, our Lord.

ALL: (Sing "Amen.")

Clothing with a White Stole

LEADER: As a sign of your newness of life through baptism, and to show that you have clothed yourself in Christ, hold your stole in your hand. Your stole shows the way you have grown in the life of Christ and the community. Place your stole on your shoulders as your name is called.

Glory to God

LEADER: Let us pray the Glory to God together.

(Selected participants ring bells or play tambourines throughout prayer.)

I will proclaim your greatness, my God. You are good to everyone and have compassion to all creation. I will praise you, God, forever and ever.

ALL: Glory to God in the highest.

LEADER: The Lord is great and is to be highly praised. Every day I will thank the Lord. I will praise you, God, forever and ever.

ALL: Glory to God in the highest.

LEADER: I will proclaim your mighty acts from one generation to the next. I will praise you, God, forever and ever.

ALL: Glory to God in the highest.

LEADER: I will tell about your goodness, Lord, and sing about your kindness. I will praise you, God, forever and ever.

ALL: Glory to God in the highest.

LEADER: People speak of your mighty deeds, Lord, and tell about your goodness.

I will praise you God, forever and ever.

ALL: Glory to God in the highest.

LEADER: The Lord is faithful to promises made. All living things look hopefully to you, Lord. I will praise you, Lord, forever and ever.

ALL: Glory to God in the highest.

(adapted from Psalm 145)

LEADER: You alone are the Lord. You alone are the most high Jesus Christ, with the Holy Spirit in the glory of God, forever and ever.

ALL: Amen.

Closing Song

ALL: (Sing the following words to the tune of "Michael, Row the Boat Ashore":)

Christ has risen as he said, Alleluia,
Christ has risen as he said, Alleluia.

We will rise again one day, Alleluia,
We will rise again one day, Alleluia.

Earth Day

A Background Reflection

The arrival of spring, signaled by the vernal equinox about March 21, has always been a time for celebration. People once believed the earth mother as having the power to bring forth green plants to the earth each year, and engaged in rites to honor her. These rites were also performed to frighten away the demons of winter and help bring in summer. People were convinced that their rites played an essential part in having the sun warm the earth for seeds to grow.

Until the Gregorian calendar was introduced in 1582, spring also marked the beginning of the New Year. One can still see a similarity in the New Year and spring rites in many cultures today.

The use of water as a symbol of health and new life originated in the earliest festivals that honored the rebirth of the natural world. According to one ancient myth, the world began in water. In many parts of Europe, women washed their faces in the spring waters of brooks and rivers for this fresh water was considered to bring new life. In the Mideast, water is used as a sign of reconciliation: wheat, celery, or lentil seeds are placed in a bowl of water. Later, they are thrown into running water as a symbolic action of doing away with all family quarrels and starting the new year in friendliness and peace.

As the four seasons are symbolic of the rhythm of human life, the season of spring becomes rebirth, resurrection after the death of winter. Every tree and bush, every blade of grass, every flower is part of the miracle of life we celebrate each spring. For Christians, Easter is the celebration of Christ rising from the dead, a joyful celebration of resurrection and eternal life. Christ takes the place of the gods in ancient mythology who died and then returned to earth to bring new life to the world. Christ brings new life to the hearts of all.

Scripture begins with the creator God fashioning an earthly dwelling for us. And each step in creating is observed and judged to be good by the Creator. Genesis gives us two versions of creation; the second story speaks of a garden (symbol of divine blessings), a tree of life in the center of the garden (ancient symbol of immortality), and a flowing river that waters this garden earth and then flows to the four directions to nourish and sustain. Not only is the enjoyment of the garden a gift from God, but God even walks in the garden, giving a yet more intimate presence. In this second creation story, we are called to be caretakers of the garden that is earth.

Centuries have passed, and still today we not only ask God to bless us but we have become acutely aware that we have not lived up to our responsibility to be stewards of earth. As caretakers of the gifts of creation, we have become remiss. Environmental groups around the world have helped make us aware of the way in which we are misusing earth and depriving people of their basic rights to clear air, water, and food produced from our garden, Earth.

In April 1970, the first Earth Day was celebrated. It was a time to reawaken a spirit of thankfulness for the earth and its goods. The theme of the day was "Give Earth a Chance," and attention was given to our responsibility to reclaim the purity of air, water, and the living environment. A special tenth anniversary of this day was observed in 1980. Although no continuing organization exists for observance, the organizers hope there will be observances of Earth Day in different places at the time of the vernal equinox every year. For example, on March 20, 1979, children rang the United Nations peace bell in New York at the exact moment the sun crossed the equator.

Earth does not belong to any one people or any one nation, but is held in trust by every generation and is passed on as a legacy. Chief Seattle of the Suquamish Nation, in delivering his speech in 1854 when he was asked to turn his

Indian tribal lands over to the federal government said,

> Care for this land as we have cared for it, and with all your strength, with all your heart, preserve it for your children and love it as God loves all. No one owns the freshness of the air and the sparkle of the water. Every part of this earth is sacred to my people. Every shining pine needle, every sandy shore, every mist in the dark woods, every clearing, and every humming insect is holy in the memory and experience of my people.

Preparations

directions

Hang the green panel for the season of spring.

Place symbols of the garden Earth from the project below on this panel.

Choose seven readers.

Place a candle and a glass bowl of water before the panel. Use an evergreen bough for dipping and sprinkling the people.

Have names ready to give as you call each participant.

materials

Construction paper, butcher paper
Magic markers
Pins
Scissors

Project

Make an earth garden for a panel (large tree, plants, vegetables, grasses, vineyards, flowers, rivers flowing in four directions, etc.) Mark the seasons. Each participant designs and prints his or her name.

Cut it out and give it to the leader.

Prayer Celebration

Opening Greeting

LEADER: We gather to celebrate the gift of the earth in spring. Rivers flow.

ALL: So be it. So be it. So be it.

LEADER: Fruit trees flower.

ALL: So be it. So be it. So be it.

LEADER: Seeds sprout green.

ALL: So be it. So be it. So be it.

LEADER: Make us aware, Lord, of the grandeur of all creation and give us feet to walk humbly and hands to touch gently this garden earth. The gifts of God's garden earth be with you.

ALL: And also with you.

Garden Earth Readings and Promises

READER 1: "The Lord planted a garden in Eden, in the east, and there put the man God had formed. God made all kinds of beautiful trees. In the middle of the garden stood the tree that gives life. A stream flowed in Eden and watered the garden; and beyond Eden divided into four rivers. Then the Lord God placed the man in the garden to cultivate and guard it. Then the Lord God said, 'It is not good for you to live alone. I will make you a suitable companion to help you.' And the Lord God made woman."

Genesis 2:8–19 (adapted)

This is the Word of the Lord.

ALL: Thanks be to God.

LEADER: We know of God's presence as creator in our garden earth. Before our creation banner, we light this candle.

(pause)

May its flame warm the earth and each of our hearts. May this burning candle be a sign of God's presence with us always. As the earth is a gift, so we, created in the image and likeness of God, we, too, are a gift. We are gardeners of the earth, caretakers of the land. We cultivate and preserve; we guard and protect. As our name is called, we come forward to receive and place a sign of ourselves in our garden earth. _____(Name)_____, you are a gift. Care for this garden earth.

(Each person receives his or her name and places it on banner.)

READER 2: In our care for this garden earth, Lord, we will make our rivers, seas, and oceans, our brooks, streams, and lakes clean and fresh again. With your help, Lord, we will let them be a source of life for flowers, trees, and fish. For we will remember, that your gift of garden earth belongs to everyone.

ALL: So be it. So be it. So be it.

READER 3: In our care for this garden earth, Lord, we will plant fruit-bearing plants and vegetables, grasses, and bright-colored flowers. In tilled soil, we will cultivate vineyards and fields of grain. And the fullness of the harvest we will share with the poor who have little. For we will remember, that your gift of garden earth belongs to everyone.

ALL: So be it. So be it. So be it.

READER 4: In our care for this garden earth, Lord, we will preserve the freshness of clean air for all to breathe. We have a right to the smells of early morning and the scents of changing seasons. For we will remember that your gift of garden earth belongs to everyone.

ALL: So be it. So be it. So be it.

READER 5: In our care for this garden earth, Lord, we will respect our bodies by eating healthy foods, becoming physically fit, avoiding harmful products. Through prayer we will nourish our spirits and try to live simply as gardeners with each other. For we will remember that your gift of garden earth belongs to everyone.

ALL: So be it. So be it. So be it.

LEADER: Lord, Thank you for the blessings of your garden earth. Inside each of us is a garden, also, a garden of your blessings. Inside each of us is the tree of life, a sign of life forever. Inside each of us the water of life, your life in us. Because of your presence may we come to know, care for, and love all the gardens of our life.

ALL: Amen.

Rite of Water

LEADER: Water is a sign of new life. A stream of life waters our garden and then flows into four rivers carrying God's life to the earth: north, south, east, and west. It is this same stream that gives drink to the city of God.

READER 6: "The river of the water of life, sparkling like crystal, flows down the middle of the city's street. On either side of the river is the tree of life, which bears fruit twelve times a year, once each month and its leaves are for the healing of the nations."

Revelations 22:1–2 (adapted)

This is the Word of the Lord.

ALL: Thanks be to God.

LEADER: We are like trees that grow beside a stream and bear fruit at the right time and whose leaves do not dry up.

READER 7: "A healthy tree does not bear bad fruit, nor does a poor tree bear good fruit. Every tree is known by the fruit it bears; you do not pick figs from thorn bushes or gather grapes from bramble bushes. A good person brings good out of the treasure of good things in her heart."

Luke 6:43–45 GNB (adapted)

LEADER: We come to our water to bless ourselves for the good fruit we will bear to others through all the months of the year.

(Water bowl is carried to each person, who dips a finger into the water and makes a self blessing in the sign of the cross; appropriate music could be played.)

Closing Blessing: Blessing of Garden Earth

LEADER: Christ is the light of our spring, the life of our garden earth, the living water that nourishes. Soon we will celebrate the paschal mystery of living, dying, and rising. At Easter, gardeners of the earth will join voices and hearts as we proclaim,
"Jesus is our Risen Lord! Alleluia!"
We bless this garden earth to receive the risen Lord. We bless all rivers.

(Dip and sprinkle water.)

ALL: Amen.

LEADER: We bless all trees.

(Dip and sprinkle water.)

LEADER: We bless all seeds.

(Dip and sprinkle water.)

ALL: Amen.

LEADER: We bless north, south, east, and west.

(Dip and sprinkle water.)

ALL: Amen.

LEADER: We bless the hearts of our faithful gardeners.

(Dip and sprinkle water.)

ALL: Amen.

LEADER: In joy and gladness, we say yes to the season of spring as we celebrate this festival of our garden earth.

ALL: So be it. So be it. So be it.

Arbor Day

A Background Reflection

Through the ages, many cultures have observed planting festivities. We, too, remember that life has been given to us as a gift, a gift we must nurture and protect. In that spirit we celebrate a national planting festival, Arbor Day, or tree day.

President Theodore Roosevelt wrote an Arbor Day letter to school children:

> It is well that you should celebrate Arbor Day thoughtfully, for within your lifetime the nation's need of trees will become serious. In your full manhood and womanhood you will want what nature once so bountifully supplied and you will reproach us not for what we have used but for what we have wasted. A people without children would face a hopeless future; a country without trees is almost as hopeless.

Once treeless, Nebraska was called the Great American Desert. Mr. and Mrs. J. Sterling Morton devoted their lives to planting trees on this barren land. Through their efforts the first Arbor Day was celebrated in Nebraska on April 10, 1872. By sundown of that first Arbor Day, Nebraskans had planted over one million trees.

People of all times have recognized the life-giving qualities of trees and the importance of taking care of our forests. England has a Garland Day; Spain celebrates the Fiesta del Arbal on March 26; Japan promotes a floral festival on April 8.

An old colonial custom required a new bride to plant a tree from her father's property beside her new home. Presidents have planted trees at the White House for posterity — elms, scarlet oaks, Japanese maples, white birches, black walnuts, magnolias. The Aztec Indians planted a tree when a baby was born and gave the baby and the tree the same name. The tree grew as the child grew toward maturity.

The Cypress in Florida, 3,000 years old, the Sequoia in the West, 3,800 years old, and the tall, majestic redwood in California standing 364 feet high inspire us to celebrate the durability and wondrous dimensions of life. The symbol of the tree of life has represented immortality in many cultures. We speak of family trees, using the tree to symbolize family relationships down through generations. We are all part of the family tree of Jesus. Rooting deep in the earth and stretching toward the sky, affected by the seasons but alive over long periods of time, the tree is a symbol of our feelings about the wonder of life itself.

Preparation

directions

Complete the project.

Choose a leader and three readers.

Choose two or three participants to plant the tree during the celebration.

Have the participants choose a name for the tree or plant.

Make necesary preparations and gather the materials for the tree-planting ceremony: small tree or plant, water, shovel or spade, flowerpot and potting soil (for indoor planting), dug hole (for outdoor planting).

Gather the participants, holding their family trees, around the planting area.

materials

items needed for tree-planting ceremony (See above.)
drawing paper
crayons or felt-tipped pens

Project

Have each participant make a family tree like the one below. Each tree should include the names of the participant's ancestors and the title "Tree of Life."

Tree of Life

Prayer Celebration

Introduction

LEADER: Let us celebrate trees — maples, oaks, sycamores, evergreen — and all other trees that remind us to look toward the future. In our planting and care of trees, we offer a sign of our gratitude to those who lived and planted before us, and we leave a sign of hope for those who will come after us. Today we celebrate the ancestors in our own family trees.

First Reading

READER 1: The Lord God said, "I am giving you all the plants and trees and seed-bearing fruits on this earth. Take good care of my garden."

(adapted from Genesis 1:29-30, 2:15)

Litany of Thanks

LEADER: For the plants of the soil,

ALL: We thank you, Lord.

LEADER: For the trees of the earth,

ALL: We thank you, Lord.

LEADER: For all seed-bearing fruit,

ALL: We thank you, Lord.

LEADER: For water, sun, and good soil that nourish growing things,

ALL: We thank you, Lord.

LEADER: For the people who care for all growing things,

ALL: We thank you, Lord.

Second Reading

READER 2: Jesus once told this story: "A man owned a fig tree which did not bear fruit. He finally said to his servant, 'Cut down this worthless tree. For three years I have looked for fruit on it, but there never is any. Why should it take up space? Cut it down.' The servant said to his master, 'Sir, let it stand for another year. I will give it special care. Then if it does not bear fruit, I will cut it down.'"

(adapted from Luke 13:6-9)

Reflection

LEADER: Let us think about the way we care for the plants and trees of this earth. Let us remember to look at trees and allow their beauty to become part of us. (Pause.)

Let us remember to leave nature as we find it when we're on outings. (Pause.)

Let us plant gardens and care for them. (Pause.)

Let us do what we can to protect trees and plants against abuse and waste. (Pause.)

Tree of Life Ceremony

LEADER: The trees of life stood on both sides of the river. Every month they bore fruit. Their leaves were used to heal people.

(adapted from Revelations 22:2)

We remember all of the people who have lived before us; we have placed their names on our family trees of life.

(If this is a family celebration, have the participants read the names written on their trees.)

We thank you, Lord, for all the people who have helped make us what we are today, your people.

Third Reading

READER 3: In the east part of Eden, God made a garden. God put many trees there. They were beautiful to behold and their fruit was good to eat. In the midst of it all stood the tree of life.

(adapted from Genesis 2:8–9)

LEADER: Lord, you are our tree of life. You nourish and strengthen us; you help us grow; you protect and care for us; continue to give us your life, so that one day we can live with you forever.

Planting and Blessing the Tree

LEADER: We plant this tree (or plant) as a sign of life, and place soil around it.

(Selected participants plant the tree.)

We name our tree＿＿＿＿＿＿.

We water the tree with this blessing:
Bless this tree.
Make it grow.
Thank you, Lord.

(If you would like to plant the tree in someone's name, do so with this blessing: "Bless this tree in the name of ＿＿＿＿＿＿. Together may they grow as God's creations.")

All the trees of the earth will shout praise before the coming of the Lord.

(adapted from Psalm 96:12-13)

Ascension Day

A Background Reflection

Ascension Day celebrates Jesus' ascent into heaven after rising from the dead. The earliest recorded observance of this feast of the Ascension was in the fourth century A.D. when it was commemorated and celebrated forty days after Easter. John Chrysostom refers to Ascension Day as an "ancient and universal" festival, and Augustine claims it originated with the apostles. Scripture tells us that Jesus "was lifted up before their eyes, and a cloud took him out of their sight" (Acts 1:9). At his Father's side, Jesus continues to pour out his spirit so that, commissioned in his love, we the people can continue to do his work in our own lives.

In medieval European villages, torches and colorful banners were carried in procession through the streets. Wells were blessed and the trellises over them were decorated with flowers. In England, the people walked the boundaries of their parishes and placed wreaths on stone property markers. The parish priest offered God's blessing for the crops. In some countries herbs and teas were gathered; there was a belief that a drink from seven kinds of herbs gave a person immunity from contagious diseases.

Since a cloud received Jesus, Ascension Day became a time for weather predictions in many places. Clouds have often been a sign of God's presence in scripture: "A cloud followed them by day to show them the way" (Exodus 13:21), and "Out of the cloud came a voice that said, 'This is my beloved son. Listen to him'" (Matthew 17:5). The cloud is also an allusion to Christ at the final coming and a prelude to the coming of the Spirit.

Perhaps we should extend those cloud-gazing moments of our youth into our adult world. Gazing at clouds can give us a meditative moment of quiet and prayer as we use our imagination to picture the delights and beauty of God's world. Living in time and space, the cloud can be welcomed as a symbol of God, as it is in scripture.

Sewing, sweeping, and working on Ascension Day were thought to bring ill fortune to the home for the remaining year. This Sabbath notion of no work on a holy day can be a sign of our anticipation of the kingdom. Instead of a work day, Ascension Day became a traditional day for mountain climbing and picnics on hilltops where cloud gazing can be done leisurely and with no distractions.

In the Western church, Ascension Day inaugurates the eight days of Ascensiontide, which last to the eve of Pentecost. In some churches the paschal candle, lighted on the eve of Easter as a symbol of the resurrected Christ, is extinguished on Ascension Day as a sign that the Light of the Word is no longer with us in his bodily presence as he once was. Rather, as the Body of Christ, the people are invited to be his light to others.

Ephesians 3:10 says that Jesus "ascended far above the heavens so that he might fill all things." The commissioning and blessing given to the disciples to preach the good news is ours also. Like the disciples, we are found together as a people of God bringing and living good news to the four corners of the earth, working for peace and justice for all men and women. While bodily presence calls attention to one place, one geographical location, the Ascension tells us of spiritual and universal presence to all people across the globe. And we are never alone, for the man Jesus who lived among us, who ate and walked with us, even though he died, is living and present among us and within us.

Preparations

directions

Hang the green panel for the season of spring. Place a candle before the panel. If using a Yule Wheel, place a candle in the center. Use four other candles on the wheel for north, south, east, west.

Choose participants to be the different people and props in the story: a mountain, a cloud, Jesus, eleven disciples (designate three for east, three for west, three for north, two for south), and alert them to the words they will be saying.

Place signs for north, south, east and west in four areas.

Prepare singing.

Choose participants for playing the drum, tambourine, and so on. Let them become familiar with the times to do so.

materials

Candles,
Drum, tambourine, etc.
Poster board, paper
Magic markers
Scissors

Prayer Celebration

Opening Greeting

LEADER: We gather to renew our hearts and spirits as together we celebrate the promise of Jesus to be with us in all that we do. Forty days have passed since Jesus rose from the dead. During this time Jesus helps the people deepen their belief in him. But now he must return to his father.

As we light this Christ candle, we remember that what Jesus did and said as he lived among us.

(Pause and light center candle.)

Together we become a part of the story of Jesus as we listen to what happened on Ascension Day.

A Scripture Presentation

(adapted and based on Matthew 28:16–20)

LEADER: There was a mountain in Galilee.

(Mountain actor appears; sound instruments.)

And to this mountain, Jesus summoned the eleven disciples. "Come this way. Come."

(Jesus gestures.)

The eleven disciples made their way up the mountain.

(eleven drum strokes as the eleven march in place)

When they saw Jesus, they fell down in homage.

(Disciples kneel and bow.)

And Jesus came forward and said,

JESUS: Full authority has been given me. Go and make disciples of all nations. Baptize them in the name of the Father and of the Son and of the Holy Spirit.

Go to the east.

(Three disciples go to the east station and say as they make the sign of the cross:)

EAST VOICES: We baptize you in the name of the Father and of the Son and of the Holy Spirit.

JESUS: Go to the west.

(Another group goes to the west station and say as they make the sign of the cross:)

WEST VOICES: We baptize you in the name of the Father and of the Son and of the Holy Spirit.

JESUS: Go to the south.

(Another group goes to the south station and say as they make the sign of the cross:)

SOUTH VOICES: We baptize you in the name of the Father and of the Son and of the Holy Spirit.

JESUS: Go to the north.

(Another group goes to the north station and say as they make the sign of the cross:)

NORTH VOICES: We baptize you in the name of the Father and of the Son and of the Holy Spirit.

JESUS: Teach them to carry out everything I have commanded you, to do my work. And disciples of the east, proclaim to everyone: Carry out the work of love.

EAST VOICES: Carry out the work of love.

ALL: We will. We will.

JESUS: And disciples of the west, proclaim to everyone: Carry out the work of caring for others.

WEST VOICES: Carry out the work of caring for others.

ALL: We will. We will.

JESUS: And disciples of the south, proclaim to everyone: Carry out the work of being kind.

SOUTH VOICES: Carry out the work of being kind.

ALL: We will. We will.

JESUS: And disciples of the north, proclaim to everyone: Carry out the work of helping others.

NORTH VOICES: Carry out the work of helping others.

ALL: We will. We will.

JESUS: And know that I am with you always, until the end of the world.

(Cloud appears and slowly moves in front of Jesus. Everyone looks up and sings to the tune of "Angels Watching Over Me.")

ALL: All night, all day,
Working for the Lord we are, we are,
All night, all day,
Working for the Lord, we are.

Psalm Response

LEADER: Men and women of __(place)__ why were you looking up into the sky?
This Jesus who has been taken up will return.
Let our response to our psalm of praise be
"Alleluia! Alleluia!"
God ascends to shouts of joy!

ALL: Alleluia! Alleulia!

LEADER: The Lord ascends to the blast of trumpets!

ALL: Alleluia! Alleluia!

LEADER: All you people clap your hands!

ALL: Alleluia! Alleluia!

LEADER: Shout to God with cries of gladness!

ALL: Alleluia! Alleulia!

LEADER: For the Lord, the most high, the Awesome one is the King over all the earth.

ALL: Alleluia! Alleulia!

LEADER: Sing praise to God, sing praise, sing praise to our king.

ALL: Alleluia! Alleulia!

LEADER: God reigns over all the nations. Sing hymns of praise.

ALL: Alleluia! Alleulia!

Psalm 47 (adapted)

Closing Blessing

LEADER: From this Christ candle we light the candles of east, west, north, and south. We extinguish the Christ candle as a sign that the Light of the World is no longer with us as he once was. Jesus invites us to be his light to others. As we look at these lights, we renew in our hearts the commission of Jesus to continue his work. We become Jesus for others and receive Jesus from others as the body of Christ. Bow your heads for God's blessing: Lord, may we follow you into the new creation. Give us voices that speak,

ALL: Give us voices that speak,

LEADER: Hands that work,

ALL: Hands that work,

LEADER: Feet that journey,

ALL: Feet that journey,

LEADER: And eyes that gaze at the splendor of your world,

ALL: And eyes that gaze at the splendor of your world.

LEADER: Your ascension, Lord, is our glory and our hope!

ALL: Alleluia! Alleulia! Alleluia!

LEADER: In the name of the Father, and of the Son, and of the Holy Spirit.

ALL: Amen.

61

Pentecost

A Background Reflection

Pentecost celebrates the presence of the Spirit in our lives. The Spirit came to the frightened apostles as they gathered behind locked doors after the resurrection. When they received the Spirit, they boldly and joyfully went forth to preach the Good News of Jesus.

Originally, Pentecost was a Jewish feast, second in importance to Passover. It focused on thanksgiving for the harvest and concluded the fifty-day Passover time. Later, Jews also celebrated the giving of the law to Moses at Sinai on Pentecost. For Christians, Pentecost recalls the descent of the Spirit upon the apostles and marks the beginning of their active work.

The symbols of the presence of the Spirit are wind, fire, and the dove. During the Middle Ages, people sometimes dramatized the Pentecost story very literally by using these symbols. Some churches had an opening in the ceiling which was called the "Holy Ghost Hole." During the Pentecost celebration, wind in the sound of trumpets or in hissing sounds made by altar boys was heard as a cart wheel, its painted underside showing a white dove, slowly descended through this hole. In some towns, burning straw was dropped to represent the tongues of fire.

Today some people light a bonfire and read the Gospel account of Pentecost. Others write the gifts of the Spirit on helium-filled balloons and release them in the ceremony to show that we are called to share our gifts with others.

John Chrysostom writes of Pentecost, "Today we have reached the capital of feasts; we have obtained the very fruit of our Lord's promise." As a custom that expresses thanks to God for fulfilling this promise, some people go to a hill or mountain in the early dawn to pray and to "catch the Spirit."

On this day, it is good to renew our baptismal promises and to celebrate the words of the Good News:

> There are different kinds of spiritual gifts, but the same Spirit gives them. . . . The Spirit's presence is shown in some way in each person for the good of all. The Spirit gives one person a message full of knowledge. . . . But it is one and the same Spirit who does all this. . . .

1 Corinthians 12:4–11

Preparation

directions

Complete the projects.

Choose a leader and two readers.

Ask each participant to choose one of the many gifts of the Spirit (wisdom, understanding, knowledge, courage, reverence, right judgment, wonder) that especially appeals to him or her. You may add other gifts if you wish.

Choose and practice a song to the Holy Spirit.

Gather the participants around a table on which you have placed the flames and the lighted candles.

materials

red Contact® paper (or red construction paper and pins)
seven candles in holders
construction paper
crayons and/or felt-tipped pens
scissors
clear plastic tape

Projects

Write these gifts of the Holy Spirit on separate strips of construction paper. Wrap each strip around a candle and tape it in place.

Have the participants use the patterns below to make flames from red Contact® paper.

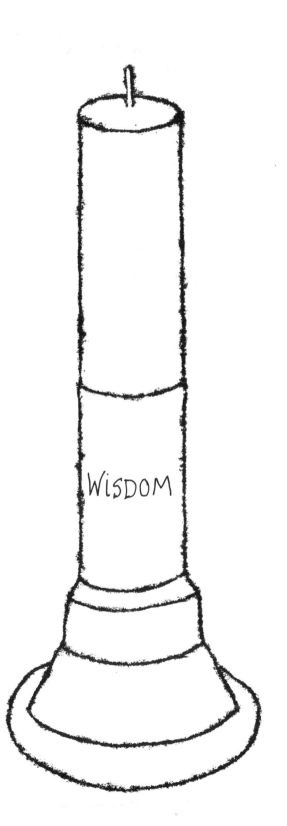

Optional: Instead of using candle holders, drill seven holes in a circular piece of wood to hold the candles. Paint the board red, if you wish, and use it yearly at Pentecost.

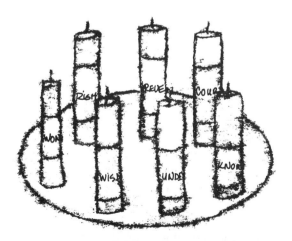

Prayer Celebration

Opening Reading

LEADER: Today we celebrate the gift of the Spirit, the gift Jesus promised to send us. The Spirit is present in all we do, renewing, encouraging, freeing, directing, and enlightening us. Let us listen to the story of the coming of the Holy Spirit.

READER 1: The disciples were all together. As they sat in the house, they heard from the sky a tremendous noise like a powerful wind. Flames like tongues of fire appeared over each of them. The Holy Spirit filled them all and they began to speak in many languages about the wonders of God.

(adapted from Acts 2:1-4)

Litany of the Gifts of the Spirit

LEADER: With the gift of wisdom, which helps us to see clearly,

(Those participants who have chosen this gift come forward and receive a flame to wear.)

ALL: Let us renew the face of the earth.

LEADER: With the gift of understanding, which helps us to know God and his people,

(Those participants who have chosen this gift come forward and receive a flame to wear.)

ALL: Let us renew the face of the earth.

LEADER: With the gift of right judgment, which helps us to make decisions,

(Those who have chosen this gift come forward and receive a flame to wear.)

ALL: Let us renew the face of the earth.

LEADER: With the gift of courage, which gives us strength and helps us not to be afraid,

(Those who have chosen this gift come forward and receive a flame to wear.)

ALL: Let us renew the face of the earth.

LEADER: With the gift of knowledge, which helps us to see our part in God's creation,

(Those who have chosen this gift come forward and receive a flame to wear.)

ALL: Let us renew the face of the earth.

LEADER: With the gift of reverence, which helps us in our just relationships with God and his people,

(Those who have chosen this gift come forward and receive a flame to wear.)

ALL: Let us renew the face of the earth.

LEADER: With the gift of wonder, which helps us to be astonished at the marvels of God,

(Those who have chosen this gift come forward and receive a flame to wear.)

ALL: Let us renew the face of the earth.

LEADER: Just as the burning bush was a sign to Moses of God's presence, the flames we wear are signs of the presence of the Spirit within each of us.

LEADER: As signs of our willingness to affirm one another in the life of the Spirit, will the parents now turn to their daughters or sons, tell them what their best gift (trait or talent) is, and then thank them for sharing that gift with others.

Now will the sons and daughters tell their parents what their best gift is and thank them for sharing that gift with others.

(In a classroom celebration, have pairs of students turn and speak to each other.)

Meditation

READER 2: You are an Alleluia. A special, unique, unrepeatable being. There never has been anyone like you and never will be. In all the millions of universes, you were made for *this* time, *this* place. How needed you are. If you were not, the world would be different. I would be different.

You are a celebration. A festival of hope, alive, a wonder. "I have come in order that you might have life, life in all its fullness."

(From "Self," a Reflection Film, Ikonographics)

Closing Song

ALL: (Sing the selected Holy Spirit song.)

Mothers' Day

A Background Reflection

In 1914, Woodrow Wilson proclaimed the second Sunday in May as Mothers' Day. He called it "a day for public expression of our love and reverence for the mothers of our country."

On the anniversary of her own mother's death in 1907, Anna Jarvis held what was probably the first service to honor all mothers. She introduced the custom of wearing a rose or a pink carnation if your mother was living, a white flower if she was dead.

Actually, Mothers' Day may have begun centuries ago. The fourth Sunday of Lent was once called "Mothering Sunday." On this day, children visited the church where they had been baptized and offered gifts to their "mother" church for the new life of baptism they had received from her. As a natural outgrowth, children brought trinkets and cakes to their own mothers, thanking them for all they had done in their children's lives.

Throughout Scripture we read of the many women who lived lives of faith and shared their faith with others — women like Judith, Deborah, Rachael, Sarah, Elizabeth, and of course Mary, the mother of Jesus.

May we celebrate the presence of mothers in our lives and show our appreciation for them by the way we live. "Let your father and mother be proud of you; give your mother that happiness" (Proverbs 23:25).

Preparation

directions

Complete the projects.

Choose two readers.

Practice an appropriate song.

Gather the participants, wearing their flowers and holding their thank-you cards, in a circle around lighted candles.

materials

pink (or rose) and white construction paper
paper doilies
pins
white paper or unlined index cards
candles, one for each participant
optional: recorded music

Projects

Have the participants use the following pattern to make flowers to wear during the celebration. (Participants whose mothers are living should use pink or rose paper; participants whose mothers are not living should use white paper.)

Have the participants make thank-you cards, using the form that is appropriate for each child.

 Thank you, Mother, for this day,

_____
(date of birth)

and for the day I was welcomed into the new life of Jesus,

_____
(date of Baptism)

I am glad you are my mother.

_____
(signature)

_____
(date of Mothers' Day this year)

 Thank you,

(Aunt Jane, Grandmother, Bette),

**for being like a mother to me.
I am glad you are my**

(aunt, grandmother, friend).

_____
(signature)

_____
(date of Mothers' Day this year)

Prayer Celebration

Introduction

LEADER: Let us celebrate all mothers — those who have lived, those now living, and those yet to live. We honor our own mothers and all women who give others life with their joy and hope.

First Reading

READER 1: I am writing now to simply tell you that I love you. I love you for your aliveness, for your joy in living, for your understanding, for your giving. You never thought of yourself in loving me. You never complained of the time I spent for others and the little time I could spend with you. And when I was discouraged and depressed, your love helped to reaffirm me, to support me in what I was doing. And when I left your home, your love freely let me go though I know you cried inside. I remember thinking when I was little, I must be someone very special that you could love me so much. You taught me how to love myself. In knowing your love I have come to love another. In knowing your love I have come to know God's love.

(from "A Letter to a Mother," Ikonographics *Love*)

LEADER: In silence, let us think of the different ways that our mothers or those who care for us have touched our lives.

(Pause.)

Thank God in your heart for this person in your life.

(Pause)

Second Reading

READER 2: Do not ask me to leave you. Let me go with you. Wherever you go I will go, wherever you live I will live, your people shall be my people, and your God my God.

(adapted from Ruth 1:16)

LEADER: In silence, reflect on how you now live for others because of your mother or those who care for you.
(Pause)

Thank God for the courage to live those actions in your life.
(Pause)

Litany of Thanks

LEADER: May we be like Ruth, faithful and loving, so that we, too, can continue to say, "Wherever you go I will go." Let us honor all mothers and all women who share life with us.

Thank you, Lord, for Eve, Sarah, Rachael, and Rebekah, the early mothers of us all.

ALL: We thank you, Lord.

LEADER: Thank you, Lord, for Judith, Deborah, and Esther, women of strength and faith.

ALL: We thank you, Lord.

LEADER: Thank you, Lord, for Ruth, Naomi, and Elizabeth, women of joy and love.

ALL: We thank you, Lord.

LEADER: Thank you, Lord, for Mary, the mother of Jesus, the woman who said yes to life.

ALL: We thank you, Lord.

LEADER: Thank you, Lord, for the mothers of each of us here.

(Names each participant. As a name is called, the participant places his or her thank-you card in front of a candle.)

ALL: We thank you, Lord. On these cards we have written our special thanks to our mothers or to other special women in our lives. We will give them our thank-you cards as signs of our love. We wear flowers as signs of our love for you, Lord, and as signs of thanksgiving for the gift of our mothers.

Closing Song

ALL: (Sing an appropriate song.)

Memorial Day

A Background Reflection

After the Civil War, Confederate families of Columbus, Mississippi, placed flowers on the graves of their loved ones and scattered flowers on the unmarked graves of both Confederate and Union soldiers. This tribute touched people of both the North and South. Later, General John Logan, Commander of the Grand Army of the Republic, designated May 30, 1868, as a day to honor the dead of the Civil War. Because the ceremonies included decorating graves, the day now called Memorial Day was originally called Decoration Day.

Today we not only honor the men and women who have been killed in war, but we remember family members and friends who have died. We plant flowers or decorate graves with flags. People hold ceremonies and parades in villages, towns, and cities across the United States. This is a day of sadness and joy — sadness for the loss of loved ones, joy that they share the new life of the resurrection.

The Tomb of the Unknown Soldier in Arlington, Virginia, was erected as a memorial to the unidentified American soldiers killed in World War I. Since Memorial Day 1958, unknown soldiers from World War II and the Korean War are also honored there. This tomb serves as the national focus for our Memorial Day celebration.

On this day we can also remember all the heroes who have formed us as a people of God. The voices of these men and women called the people to remember to live as the people of God. Sometimes we find, in what people are willing to die for, what we choose to live for.

Within all men and women, there is a yearning for unity and peace, a yearning for reconciliation. God does not belong to any one nation, but to all people. Together we recognize and celebrate our common humanity, and we remember the men and women who have died that we might live more freely. We pray for God's universal reign of peace in the words of the prophet Micah:

> He will settle disputes among the nations,
>   among the great powers near and far.
> They will hammer their swords into plows
>   and their spears into pruning knives.
> Nations will never again go to war,
>   never prepare for battle again.
> Everyone will live in peace among
>   his own vineyards and fig trees,
>   and no one will make him afraid.
> The Lord Almighty has promised this.

Micah 4:3-4

Preparation

directions

Complete the project.

Choose a leader and a reader for the closing prayer.

Practice singing "We Will Walk to that Glory Land" or other appropriate songs.

Gather the participants outside and have them stand in a circle holding their flowers. Before the celebration begins, ask the participants to think for a few moments about people important to them who have died.

If possible, visit a cemetery after the celebration and place the flowers there.

materials

construction paper in assorted colors
wooden sticks or dowels
a stapler or tape

Project

Have the participants use the following patterns to make construction-paper flowers and leaves. Staple or tape each flower and two leaves to a wooden stick or dowel.

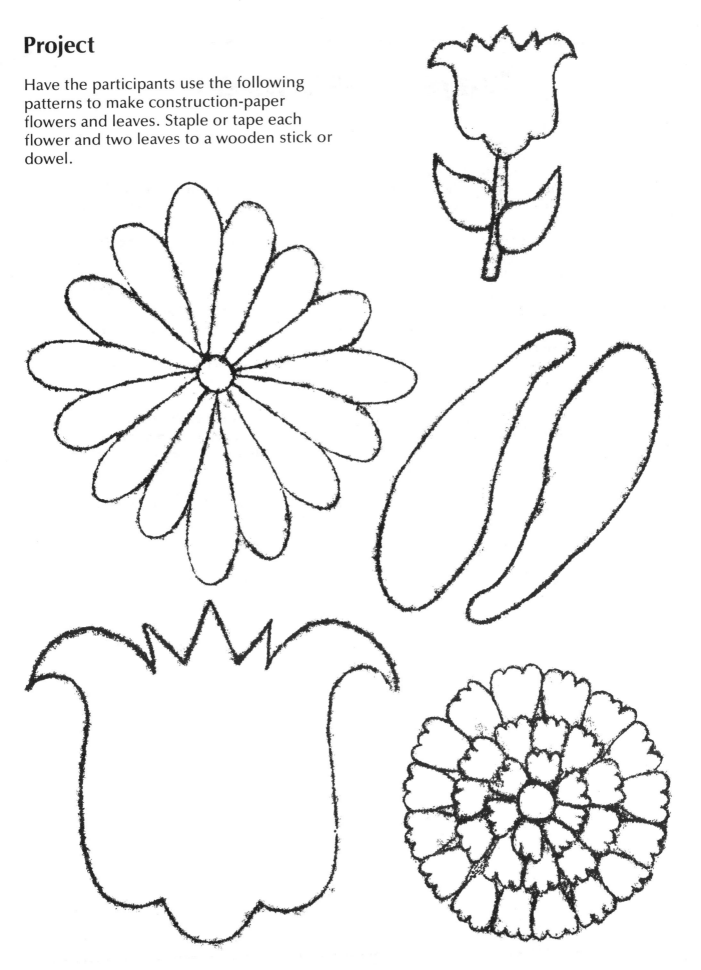

Prayer Celebration

Introduction

LEADER: Fourscore and seven years ago our fathers brought forth on this continent a new nation, conceived in liberty, and dedicated to the proposition that all men are created equal.... We have come to dedicate a portion of that field as a final resting place for those who here gave their lives that that nation might live... The world will little note, nor long remember, what we say here, but it can never forget what they did here. It is for us, the living, rather to be dedicated here to the unfinished work...that this nation, under God, shall have a new birth of freedom — and that government of the people, by the people, for the people, shall not perish from the earth.

(excerpted from *The Gettysburg Address*, Abraham Lincoln)

ALL: (Sing "Where Have all the Flowers Gone?")

Prayer for a New World

LEADER: The Lord says, "I am making a new heaven and a new earth. The new Jerusalem will be full of joy; her people will be happy."

ALL: I am making a new heaven and a new earth.

LEADER: "No one there will weep; no one will need to call for help."

ALL: I am making a new heaven and a new earth.

LEADER: "Like trees, my people will live long lives. They will enjoy the things that they work for."

ALL: I am making a new heaven and a new earth.

LEADER: "I will bless my people for all time to come. Before they finish praying to me, I will answer their prayers."

ALL: I am making a new heaven and a new earth.

(adapted from Isaiah 65:17)

LEADER: Lord, we thank you for this promise of a new heaven and a new earth. We thank you for the men and women who, like your Son, have given up their lives for us. We thank you

for David, Joshua, Peter; (Pause.)

for Abraham Lincoln, Robert E. Lee, Ulysses S. Grant; (Pause.)

for John F. Kennedy, Martin Luther King, Jr., Robert Kennedy; (Pause)

for all those who have died in wars; (Pause.)

for all those whom we know and those we don't know. (Pause.)

We remember our own family and friends who have gone before us in the sign of faith. We remember:

(Participants mention names of people they want to remember as they raise their flowers gently into the air.)

Closing Prayer

LEADER: Let us now listen to our closing prayer.

READER: Our earth is but a small star in the great universe. Yet of it we can make, if we choose, a planet unvexed by war, untroubled by hunger or fear, undivided by senseless distinctions of race, color, or theory.

Grant us brotherhood, not only for this day but for all our years — a brotherhood not of words but of acts and deeds. We are all of us children of earth — grant us that simple knowledge. If our brothers and sisters are oppressed, then we are oppressed. If they hunger, we hunger. If their freedom is taken away, our feedom is not secure.

Grant us a common faith that we shall know bread and peace — that we shall know justice and righteousness, freedom and security, an equal opportunity and an equal chance to do our best, not only in our own lands but throughout the world. And in that faith, let us march toward the clean world our hands can make.

("Prayer for a Better World" by Stephen Vincent Benet, written for and read by President Franklin D. Roosevelt to the United Nations on Flag Day, June 14, 1942)

LEADER: Let us place our flowers in the earth as signs that like the men and women who have lived before us we will work together to make a new world.

ALL: (Sing "We Will Walk to That Glory Land" or another appropriate song.)

Fathers' Day

A Background Reflection

As kind as a father is to his children, so is the Lord to those who honor him.

Psalm 103:13

In the United States we celebrate Fathers' Day on the third Sunday in June. This is a day to remember all of the fathers in our lives, to honor them, and to give thanks for them.

In 1909, Mrs. John Bruce Dodd, wanting to honor her own father, persuaded the Ministerial Society of Spokane, Washington, to have a special church service for all fathers. The first public celebration was held the following year. By 1924, President Calvin Coolidge recommended a national observance, "to establish more intimate relations between fathers and their children, and to impress upon fathers the full measure of their obligations." In the United States, the red or white rose has been selected as the official Fathers' Day flower.

In Czechoslovakia, children tie their father to a chair and sing, "Fathers' Day, Fathers' Day, what will you give?" Only after the father has given a gift will the children untie him. For most people, the very presence of our fathers in our lives, or the memory of our fathers, is a gift.

This is a day for all fathers, for all guardians, for all men who stand as a spiritual parent to another. We remember the fathers of our heritage — patriarchal fathers, church fathers, pilgrim fathers, fathers of the constitution, grandfathers and great-grandfathers — all men who give us care and guidance, protection and love.

Teachers, neighbors, friends can also be fathers to us. By being father to one, these men become fathers to all. As Jesus called God Father, so we, too, on this day can choose to give thanks for God's presence as Father in the life of Jesus and in our own lives.

Preparation

directions

Complete the project.

Choose participants for the readings — a child for the first reading, a man for the second, if possible. Be sensitive to those who do not have fathers. Emphasize that this celebration is for all men who care for us.

materials

an old hat belonging to father of the
    participants (for a family
    celebration)
construction paper
scissors
crayons
glue or clear plastic tape

Project

Have the participants make symbols from construction paper of important events and things that children and fathers share. For a family celebration, have the participants attach these symbols to one of their father's old hats. For a classroom celebration, have the participants attach their symbols to construction-paper hats.

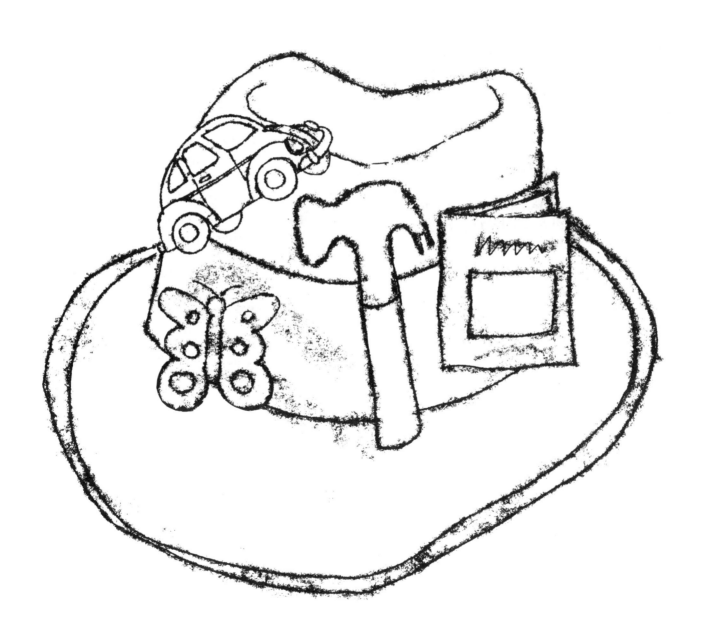

Prayer Celebration

Introduction

LEADER: We come together to celebrate a day for fathers. Today we show our appreciation for all the men in our lives who give us care and protection, love and direction. It is a day to celebrate as brothers and sisters and to call God Father, as Jesus did.

A Remembering Hat

LEADER: Different hats represent different things people do with their lives.

(Participants present hat(s) to their father(s).)

On this (these) hat(s) we have put signs of what you have shared and lived with us.

(Optional: Have the participants tell about their symbols.)

Readings

READER 1: Children, pay attention to your father. The Lord has set the father up as head of his family. Honor your father in everything you do so that his blessings will rest on you, for a father's blessing is what makes a family secure. Take care of your father when he is old. Kindness to a father will not be overlooked. Fathers, be good to your children. Raise them to be loving children of God.

(adapted from Ephesians 6:4)

READER 2: Listen carefully, children, to a father's good advice. Do not forget what I tell you. These are the same things that my father told me. He said, "Keep my words in your heart and obey my commandments so that you may have life." He told me to find knowledge and understanding. Watch your tongue that you do not speak lies or trickery. Be straightforward in all you do. Keep on the right path, avoiding evil carefully. If you pay attention to my words, the years of your life will be many.

(adapted from Proverbs 1-5, 24-26)

The Fathers' Litany

ALL: Lord, God, may your blessing come upon us.

LEADER: God, you are Father to all of us, you have made us in your image.

ALL: Lord, God, may your blessing come upon us.

LEADER: Patriarchal fathers — Abraham, Isaac and Jacob — in faith and hope you lived the promise for us.

ALL: Lord, God, may your blessing come upon us.

LEADER: Church fathers — Gregory, Augustine, Jerome, Ambrose — with others you guide us in wisdom.

ALL: Lord, God, may your blessing come upon us.

LEADER: Pilgrim fathers, you came to a new land and formed America for us.

ALL: Lord, God, may your blessing come upon us.

LEADER: Fathers of the Constitution, you united us and gave us hope to be one free people.

ALL: Lord, God, may your blessing come upon us.

LEADER: Our fathers, grandfathers and great-grandfathers, you cared for us and gave each of us a personal past, a personal heritage.

ALL: Lord, God, may your blessing come upon us.

LEADER: Thank you, God, for giving us these fathers. Through them we remember we are one family, sharing a common past and living toward a common future.

Final Blessing

LEADER: I speak for all fathers as I ask you to bow your heads.

(adapted from Ephesians 6:4)

(Extends hands over everyone.)

I love you all. May we grow together in knowing and loving one another. May you always love. Thank you for loving me.

Now let us sing!

ALL: He's got the whole world in his hands....

He's got all of the fathers in his hands....

He's got all of the children in his hands....

Independence Day

A Background Reflection

On the Fourth of July, we celebrate the formal adoption by the Continental Congress of the Declaration of Independence, which announced the American colonies' freedom from Great Britain. Communities across our nation mark this day with athletic contests, picnics, patriotic programs, parades, and fireworks.

In 1776, John Adams wrote to his wife Abigail: "I am apt to believe that this day will be celebrated by succeeding generations...with pomp and parade, with shows, games, sports, guns, bells, bonfires and illuminations, from this time forevermore." How right he was!

Early celebrations of Independence Day recalled not only our history as a nation but also our history as a nation turned toward God. The names of Moses, David, and Isaiah were linked with those of John Adams, Thomas Jefferson, and Benjamin Franklin when people spoke of our right to be free. This religious attitude pervades the often-quoted part of the Declaration of Independence: "We hold these truths to be self-evident, that all men (women) are created equal, that they are endowed by their Creator with certain inalienable rights, that among these are life, liberty, and the pursuit of happiness."

Jesus came so that we may be free. "Freedom is what we have. Christ has set us free" (Galatians 5:1). Freedom is our Christian as well as our national inheritance.

The Liberty Bell summoned the people to the proclamation of our independence in 1776. The words imprinted on its rim are important to us today as Christians and as citizens: "Proclaim liberty throughout all the land unto all the inhabitants thereof."

We rejoice in the gifts God has given us and together declare:

My country 'tis of thee,
Sweet land of liberty,
Of thee I sing.
Land where my Fathers died
Land of the pilgrims' pride
From every mountain side
Let freedom ring.

"America," Samuel Francis Smith

Preparation

directions

Complete the projects.

Select a leader and two readers.

Practice singing "America" and one other patriotic song such as "Yankee Doodle" or "It's a Grand Old Flag."

Optional: Prepare a picnic lunch or supper to precede the prayer celebration.

Gather the participants, wearing their freedom armbands, in a circle around the scroll and the flag.

materials

a large sheet of shelf paper
construction paper in assorted colors
scissors
paste or glue
crayons or felt-tipped markers
tape
an American flag

Projects

Make a scroll like this one. Have the participants declare the rights of free people and then sign their names.

OUR UNANIMOUS DECLARATION OF INDEPENDENCE

When in the course of human events it becomes necessary to declare:

(Write in this space the rights of people which the group feels are important.)

And for the support of this Declaration, with a firm reliance on the protection of Divine Providence, we mutually pledge to each other our lives, our fortunes, and our sacred honor. We sign our names on this day, in the year of our Lord, nineteen hundred and (this year's date).

Signed: (All sign here.)

Have each participant draw or paste a freedom symbol on a strip of construction paper to make a freedom armband.

 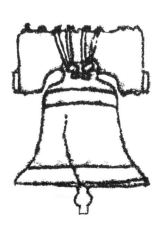 

Prayer Celebration

Introduction

LEADER: We gather together to declare our freedom as a people of God, our freedom as citizens of the United States of America.

ALL: (Sing "America.")

First Reading

READER 1: Hear, O Israel! The Lord is our God, the Lord alone. You shall love the Lord, your God, with all your heart and with all your strength. Listen to these words and remember them. Teach them to your children. Speak of them wherever you are, whether you are busy or at rest. Wear them on your wrists and foreheads as signs of your faithfulness. Write them on the doorposts of your houses and on your gates.

(adapted from Deuteronomy 6:4-9)

LEADER: The laws God gave the people through Moses are gifts — gifts that make us free to love God, free to love God's people. On our arms we wear signs of our freedom.

(The participants name their signs, as they hold their arms up high.)

Second Reading

READER 2: We, the people of the United States, in order to form a more perfect Union, establish justice, insure domestic tranquility, provide for the common defense, promote the general welfare, and secure the blessings of liberty to ourselves and our posterity, do ordain and establish this Constitution for the United States of America.

(Preamble of the Constitution of the United States of America)

LEADER: The rights that our nation states in her Constitution are gifts that help us live in respect and responsibility with one another. The Shema, the Jewish profession of faith, was written on a scroll and read daily in the temple. Similarly, we read this scroll which states our belief.

ALL: (Read the scroll together and then state their names individually.)

Litany of Freedom

LEADER: With the Unted Nations, let us declare the human rights of all people, of all countries, and let us remember that we are not free until all people are free.

ALL: We are not free until all people are free.

LEADER: Everyone has the right to freedom of thought, of conscience, and of religion.

ALL:	We are not free until all people are free.
LEADER:	Everyone has the right to freedom of opinion and expression.
ALL:	We are not free until all people are free.
LEADER:	Everyone has the right to take part in the government of his or her country.
ALL:	We are not free until all people are free.
LEADER:	Everyone has the right to work.
ALL:	We are not free until all people are free.
LEADER:	Everyone has the right to rest and leisure.
ALL:	We are not free until all people are free.
LEADER:	Everyone has the right to a standard of living adequate to the needs of person and family.
ALL:	We are not free until all people are free.
	(adapted from the Declaration of Human Rights, General Assembly of the United Nations, December 10, 1948)
LEADER:	We celebrate the rights of all people to be free. We promise to work to free the world from violence, tyranny, oppression, ignorance, starvation. We know from the Scriptures that "Freedom is what we have, Christ has set us free."

Pledge to the Flag

LEADER:	Let us stand and say together a pledge of freedom.
ALL:	I pledge allegiance to the flag of the United States of America and to the republic for which it stands, one nation under God, indivisible, with liberty and justice for all.
	(Pledge to the Flag, Francis Bellamy)

Closing Song

ALL:	(Sing "Yankee Doodle," "It's a Grand Old Flag," or another patriotic song.)

Labor Day

A Background Reflection

Work brings dignity and self worth to our lives. In our work, we do more than make a living; we make a life. With work we share in God's plan of bringing order out of chaos. Through our work, we are invited to take part in the ongoing task of creation, of building the earth.

Work also relates to our attitude toward our country. Many of our presidents felt proud to say that they once earned a living by working with their hands. People say that our nation rose up from the labor of her people. To celebrate work and workers, President Cleveland in 1894 declared the first Monday in September as Labor Day, a national and legal holiday.

Working conditions have not always been what they are today. To protest miserable working conditions, poor salaries, and long working hours, workers organized labor unions. These unions protected the rights of the laborers and helped to fulfill some of their needs. In 1882, Peter J. McGuire, President of the Carpenter's Brotherhood, proposed to the Central Labor Union of New York that a day for labor be observed throughout the United States, "to honor the industrial spirit, the great vital force of the nation." People organized parades and marches for improved working conditions, and workers held a variety of festivities. Then in 1894, Labor Day became a national holiday.

On Labor Day, we celebrate work and the worker. We also reflect on ways to help all people find the work for which they are suited or to help them develop skills to find work. In this celebration we remember that

> Everything you do or say, then, should be done in the name of the Lord Jesus. . . .

Colossians 3:17

Preparation

directions

Complete the project.

Choose a leader and three readers.

Practice singing "This Land Is Your Land" or another appropriate song or chant.

Gather the participants outside, if possible. Rest the signs along the wall of your home or school until they are needed in the celebration.

materials

cardboard, oak tag, or posterboard
felt-tipped pens or crayons
flat wooden sticks or reasonably straight
  branches
a stapler

Project

Have the participants decide on the workers they wish to support and make signs like those below. Staple the completed signs to sticks or branches.

83

Prayer Celebration

Introduction

LEADER: We are the caretakers of the land. Together we work to build the earth. Today we celebrate both ourselves as workers and the work we do.

First Reading

READER 1:   "I am putting you in charge of the fish, the birds, the wild animals, and all living things. I give you grain and all kinds of fruit for your food. For the wild animals and for the birds I have provided grass and leafy plants."

God looked at all that he had made and saw that it was very good.

(adapted from Genesis 1:28-31)

LEADER: God gives us different gifts to do different work. Help us to choose our work according to our gifts, Lord.

Second Reading

READER 2:   If our gift is to speak God's message, we should do it according to the faith that we have. If it is to serve, we should serve; if it is to teach, we should teach; if it is to encourage others, we should do so. Whoever shares with others should do so generously; whoever has authority over others should rule with care; whoever shows kindness to others should do so cheerfully.

(adapted from Romans 12:6-8)

LEADER: In our jobs, we do our best; we finish what we have started; we do all work in your name, Lord.

Third Reading

READER 3:   Well done, good and faithful servant. Since you have been faithful over a little, I will put you in charge of more important matters. Come and share your master's joy.

(adapted from Matthew 25:23)

LEADER: We celebrate our completed tasks and thank you, God, for helping us to be competent in the work we do.

I Hear America Singing, a Litany

LEADER: I hear America singing, the varied carols I hear,

Those of the mechanics, each singing a song that should be blithe and strong.

ALL: At your work, O Lord, we sing your praise.

LEADER: The weaver singing as the long, colorful strands rise and fall.

ALL: At your work, O Lord, we sing your praise.

LEADER: The typist singing as the machine hums and clicks.

The doctors and nurses singing of their care for the weak and sick.

ALL: At your work, O Lord, we sing your praise.

LEADER: The potter singing as the wheel spins, the hatter singing at the assembly line.

The wood-cutter's song, the farmer's in the field, the teacher's on the way to school.

ALL: At your work, O Lord, we sing your praise.

LEADER: Each sings what belongs to him or her and to none else.

ALL: At your work, O Lord, we sing your praise.

LEADER: Lord, may we hear all people singing across the earth as they work to make a new world. Help us respect the work we do and the work that others do.

(based on ''I Hear America Singing'' by Walt Whitman)

Work Pledge

LEADER: Repeat after me our pledge of work:

We promise to work hard

ALL: We promise to work hard

LEADER: to make a new world

ALL: to make a new world

LEADER: and to thank people

ALL: and to thank people

LEADER: for the work they do

ALL: for the work they do

LEADER: in your name, God, maker of all creation.

ALL: in your name, God, maker of all creation.

March in Support of Workers

LEADER: Let us take up our signs and proclaim our support of the different kinds of work that people do in our land.

(Participants name in turn the workers they support as they raise their signs.)

Let us show our support for the workers of the world by carrying our signs.

(As you march around the school or home, sing ''This Land Is Your Land'' or any appropriate song.)

Native Americans' Day

A Background Reflection

Thousands of years before Christopher Columbus reached the western hemisphere, the American Indians made their homes in North and South America. Living simply, they fished and hunted where modern cities now stand, guided canoes quietly along rivers now crowded with ships. With reverence for nature and an intimate relationship with every living creature, they dwelled as community in family and tribe not only with the living but with a deep respect for deceased relatives and friends.

In their celebrations, the Indians emphasized ritual, symbol, and nonverbal communication. The important thing in a ceremony was movement, the dance. Dance conveyed an idea to the spirits and was not performed for the pleasure of an audience. A beating of drums and a shaking of rattles accompanied the movement.

For the Indians, nature was not something outside themselves to be exploited; rather, they felt themselves to be part of nature and honored the gods as found in woods, animals, or the earth. Chief Mountain Lake of the Taos Pueblos said, "We are a people who live on the roof of the world; we are the sons and daughters of Father Sun and with our religion we daily help our father go across the sky. We do this not only for ourselves, but for the whole world. If we were to cease practicing our religion, in ten years the sun would no longer rise. Then it would be night forever." These Indians believed they were partners with God, preserving and sustaining God's gift of creation for all people. We are reminded of Gensis, where God asks that we become stewards and caretakers of the earth.

Because the Indians were so intimately bonded to the land, their ritual ceremonies paralleled their hunting, or their planting and harvesting of the first fruits. Mother Earth, Father Sun, Sister Rain—all were praised and thanked. The seedtime, growth, and harvest of the corn was depicted in a variety of rites and ritual dances. The *kiva*, an underground room for religious ceremonies, welcomed the men of the village. After the ceremony, prayer sticks, lengths of wood with feathers attached, were taken back to their dwellings for continued communication with the spirits. The eternal pattern of seedtime, growth, ripe fruit in the sunshine, rain, and the good harvest was repeated each year.

We are reminded of the scriptural parables of the kingdom shown in the stories of the sower and the farmer and the patterns of seeding, growing, and harvesting. Like the American Indians, we know that though we sow and reap, it is still God who has made the seed grow and has brought it to harvest.

There were many, diverse Indian tribes. Some lived by hunting and gathering nuts, seeds, and roots; others planted gardens. Some made their dwellings in teepees, other in adobe homes. In North America alone, there was once over 300 tribal languages and countless dialects.

By the time the white settlers came to America, our native Americans had explored almost all the land, discovered important natural resources, found the easiest trails over mountains and across rivers. As newcomers, the settlers were guided by the Indians to mineral springs and mineral deposits, shown how to travel by canoe and snowshoes, and taught how to grow food. Having developed wild plants into useful food through thousands of years of cultivation, the settlers were shown how to cook the food. And throughout the bitter cold winters of the settlers' early years when food was scarce, the Indians were generous in offering their own food.

As settlers went westward, the Indians were forced farther away from their homelands. When they stopped to defend themselves, they were forcibly overwhelmed by the whites. Banding together under leaders like King Philip, Pontiac, and Tecumseh, they were overcome again not only by their opponents but in the realization of how different they were as individual tribes. The defeated Indians were placed on reservation lands that had little or no value.

In 1915, at the annual assembly of the American Indian Association, over a thousand Indians representing more than a hundred tribes voted approval of an annual American Indian Day. Sherman Coolidge, an Arapahoe Indian and president of the assembly, urged recognition of Indian citizenship and Indian loyalty: "We declare our needs now and tomorrow as those primarily of Americans struggling for enlightenment and competency that are consistent with American citizenship. May this day be observed as a memorial to the Indian race and to a wise consideration of its future as part of the American people." Today, most states celebrate Native American Day on the fourth Friday in September. Some states observe this day on the second Saturday in May or select a day during the year convenient for all residents.

The Indians' road to citizenship in a country where they had lived all their lives was slow and arduous. Only in 1924 was citizenship granted to all Indians born in the United States, and only by 1948 were American Indians finally able to vote in all states.

Throughout our country, we have reminders of America's roots in an Indian culture—thousands of Indian names of rivers, towns, cities, and states, as well as the words and concepts that are now part of our everyday speech, such as *toboggan, tobacco, moccasin,* and *raccoon.* Indian foods are still eaten today: succotash, hominy, squash. Today many societies and museums throughout the country, such as the Institute of American Indian Art in New Mexico, the Museum of the American Indian in New York, offer in their collections the richness and variety of Indian culture and their contribution to the formation of our own culture.

Preparations

directions

Hang the orange panel for the season of fall.

Choose six readers. Choose a narrator or let the leader do this part also.

Place four candles to form a circle (or, if you have a Yule Wheel, use it). Indicate north, south, east, and west for each candle. Place the Wheel before the panel.

Choose people to use prayer sticks and other sounds.

Choose people to present the sun, green shoots, blades, grain ears, ripe grain.

Show all participants the movement for each part of the parable of the farmer. This movement is to give them an experience of a ritual pattern as expressed by American Indians in dance.

materials

Orange panel
Yule Wheel
Candles
Prayer sticks
Sound makers
Construction paper
Magic markers
Scissors
Ribbons, feathers
Pins or tape

Project

Make a sign for each of earth's directions: north, south, east, west.

Make a sun, green shoots, blades, green ears of grain, ripe grain.

Make prayer sticks (use branches found outdoors). Put ribbons, feathers, and strips of paper on them.

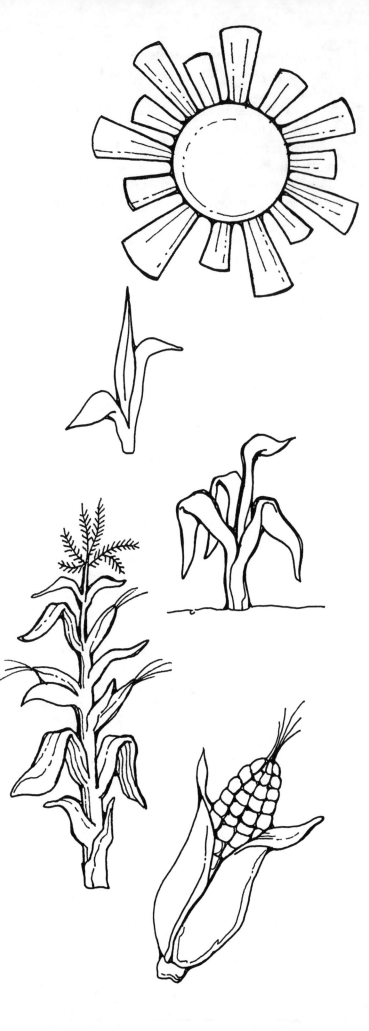

Prayer Celebration

Opening Greeting

LEADER: We gather to give thanks and recognition to our native Americans. We thank God for their presence on our planet Earth and for showing us how to respect all of life. The Spirit of God be with you.

ALL: And also with you.

LEADER: Let us listen to the plea of an Arapahoe Indian for a day of recognition for our native Americans.

READER 1: "We do invite all Americans who love their country and would uphold its honor and dignity, to celebrate this day and to consider our early philosophy, our love of freedom, our social institutions, and our history in the full light of truth and the balance of justice, in honest comparison with the annals of other races and to draw therefrom these noble things that we believe are worthy of emulation. We call upon our country to consider the past, but to earnestly consider our present and our future as a part of the American people. To them we declare our needs now and tomorrow as those primarily of Americans struggling for enlightment."
Sherman Coolidge, an Arapahoe

Proclamation at the Assembly
of the American Indian Association 1915

LEADER: The wheel stands as a way of life. Within its circle one sees all people as a whole.

READER 2: At the place of north we light this candle in thanksgiving for the Chippewa, Sioux, Cree, Cheyenne, Winnebago, Ottawa, Crow, Blackfoot, Chinook, Shoshoni, Comanche, Dakota.

(pause and do so)

READER 3: At the place of west, we light this candle in thanksgiving for the Arapahoe, Pueblo, Apache, Navaho, Hopi, Ute, Maidu, Pomo, Yuma, Mohave.

(pause)

READER 4: At the place of south, we light this candle in thanksgiving for the Seminole, Cherokee, Shawnee, Chickasaw, Creek, Chocktaw, Natchez, Quapaw, Tuscarora.

(pause)

READER 5: At the place of east, we light this candle in thanksgiving for the Delaware, Mohegan, Iroquois, Mohawk, Cayuga, Oneida, Seneca, Narraganset, Algonquin, Massachuset.

(pause)

The One Journey

LEADER: We are one people. Like our native Americans, we invite and welcome the ancients, our invisible companions, as guests in our daily living. We remember all people who have walked this earth from the beginning of time

(pause—sound of prayer sticks)

and we welcome them as guests for our journey of life. We remember all family members who have died, those most recent and those of long ago

(pause—sound of prayer sticks)

and we welcome them as guests for our journey of life. We remember Jesus and the promise of his spirit with us always.

(pause—sound of prayer sticks)

and we welcome this spirit as guest for our journey of life.
Lord, our God,
God of our mothers and fathers,
God of Abraham and Sarah,
God of Isaac and Rebecca,
God of Jacob and Rachel,
be present with us now as we gently walk your earth and touch with reverence your creation. We welcome you, and all people that you have made into our hearts. May we be guests to one another. We ask this of you as creator and sustainer of all life.

(pause—sound of prayer sticks)

ALL: Amen.

Rite of Growing

LEADER: Scripture teaches us about the Kingdom of God in the pattern of seeding, growing, and harvesting. We learn from our native Americans a respect and reverence for this pattern expressed in their dance rituals.

NARRATOR: One day the sun was shining brightly.

(gesture, sound—sun is placed on panel)

And a farmer went out and scattered seed on the ground.

(gesture, sound—seed placed on panel)

The farmer prays for rain.

(gesture, sound)

The farmer goes to bed and sleeps.

(gesture, sound)

The farmer awakens at day

(gesture, sound)

and sleeps at night.

(gesture, sound)

And through all those nights and days, the seed begins to sprout of their own accord. First, the shoot,

(gesture, sound—shoot placed on panel)

then the blades,

(gesture, sound—blade placed on panel)

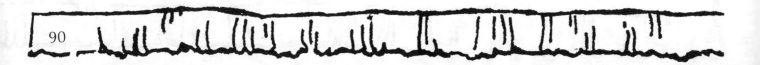

then the ear,

(gesture, sound—ear placed on panel)

and then the full grain in the ear.

(gesture, sound—grain placed on panel)

And when the crop is ready, the farmer begins to reap for the time of harvest has come.

(gesture, sound)

Based on Mark 4:26-29

LEADER: We remember from this story that though we may sow the seed and reap, still it is God who has made the seed to grow and has brought it to the harvest. It takes time and patience for the Kingdom of God to grow. In our journey together, we, too, are seeds, we are the kingdom that is daily growing.

Lord,
Give us sun to warm our hearts and rain to nourish our spirits so we may growing in your likeness. Our response will be, "Lord, we are the work of your hands. Let us know that wherever we are in our growing, it is a good and holy place to be.
Lord, we are the work of your hands."

ALL: Lord, we are the work of your hands.

LEADER: Give us honest acceptance of who we are and who others are in relation to us.
"Lord, we are the work of your hands."

ALL: Lord, we are the work of your hands.

LEADER: Give us sleep at night and wakefulness during the day as we live your life for others.
"Lord, we are the work of your hands."

ALL: Lord, we are the work of your hands.

LEADER: Let us know the time of planting, of reaping, and of harvesting and give us patience to see the time as your time.
"Lord, we are the work of your hands."

ALL: Lord, we are the work of your hands.

Closing Blessing

LEADER: Let us sit. Become quiet inside. We are the inner circle of the wheel, we are one, we are the people of God. As God's people, let us close our eyes and listen to the Spirit through the words of the Plains Indians.

READER 6: "Come sit with me and let us smoke the Pipe of Peace in Understanding. Let us touch. Let us, each to the other, be a Gift as is the Buffalo. Let us be Meat to Nourish each other, that we may all Grow. Sit here with me, each of you as you are in your own Perceiving of yourself. Let me see through your Eyes. Let us teach each other here in this great Lodge of the people, this Sun Dance, of each of the Ways on this Great Medicine Wheel, our earth."

Seven Arrows, Hyemeyohsts Storm

LEADER: Lift your hands, hearts, and heads for God's blessing. May we be gift.

ALL: Amen.

LEADER: May we nourish each other for growth.

ALL: Amen.

LEADER: May we learn the ways of God's earth.

ALL: Amen.

LEADER: We go forth in peace. In our homes we place our prayer sticks. May they daily remind us of God's spirit in all the moments of our daily living and growing. In the name of God the Creator, the Son the Redeemer, and the Spirit the Giver of Life.

ALL: Amen.

Columbus Day

A Background Reflection

"Land! Land!" After thirty-three days of crossing unknown seas, these words brought rejoicing to the crew and captain of the three small Spanish ships, the *Nina*, the *Pinta*, and the *Santa Maria*. On reaching shore, Christopher Columbus knelt and thanked God for a safe voyage. From Columbus's journal, we read this entry: "Friday, 12th of October. . . . The admiral took and planted on the earth the royal standard with two other banners of the green cross. These two banners had an *F* and a *Y* (Fernando and Ysabel) and a crown over each letter, one on one side of the cross, and the other on the other side. We saw trees very green, and much water, and fruits of diverse kinds."

Columbus felt that divine guidance was with him in all his explorations. His faith gave him the courage to enter unknown territory. Confident in his belief that Earth was round, Columbus was determined to find a short route to India. Since he miscalculated Earth's size and did not realize that the ocean surrounding Japan was not the same as the one along the shores of Spain, he persisted in his belief that he had reached the Indies and returned in triumph to Spain and to his benefactors.

Born in Genoa, Italy, Columbus was a self-taught man, persuasive in his beliefs; a capable sea commander; and a careful and accurate navigator. He discovered the best way to use winds for transatlantic sailing, began the European settlement of the West Indies, and made the first European exploration of South America and the western Caribbean. He made four voyages in all to this "new world" but he found none of the spices and wealth of the Indies for which he was searching.

An Italian, Americus Vespucius, who explored the coast of South America after Columbus, told thrilling stories of his voyages. As these stories circulated, a German map maker identified the new land on his map by printing the word "America" across it.

Columbus reminds us of the courage it takes to travel new roads and the confidence that is needed to begin our travel. We are reminded of the call of God to Abraham and Sarah to leave their homeland and travel to a new land. That same call comes to each of us. It is a call not only to travel in the space we know but to take the unknown inner journey to discover who we each are as persons and who together we might be as a people. Let us make our land a home where freedom, peace, and justice are for all people. In the words of the poet Lord Tennyson, "Let us seek and strive for a better world."

Preparations

directions

Hang the orange panel for season of spring.

Choose three readers.

Place a candle in front of the panel.

On the orange panel, display the flag Columbus planted in America.

Display a map of America.

Have family signs ready for participants to place on American map.

materials

Orange panel
American map
Construction paper
Magic markers
Scissors
Pins or tape
Candle

Project

On the orange panel, make a cross with a crown in each of the top portions of the letters *F* and *Y* in each of the lower portions.

Outline a map of America.

Each participant chooses and makes a family sign. He or she will place these signs on the map for places where the family has lived or traveled.

Prayer Celebration

Opening Greeting

LEADER: This is the land of America. Long ago, one man, Christopher Columbus, reached far beyond the world he lived in. With courage and confidence, he sailed in search of a new land, a land that became a home for people of all nations who would one day also leave their homelands. How does one trust the vision? Where does one find the courage? How does one reach beyond the known? We listen to the poet for the faith that is needed to light unknown paths.

READER 1: "O, World, thou choosest not the better part.
It is not wisdom to be only wise,
And on the inward vision close the eye.
But it is wisdom to believe the heart.
Columbus found a world, and had no chart,
Save one that faith deciphered in the skies;
To trust the soul's invincible surmise
Was all his science and his only art.
Our knowledge is a torch of smoky pine
That lights the pathway but one step ahead
Across a void of mystery and dread.
Bid the tender light of faith to shine
By which alone the moral heart is led
Unto the thinking of the thought divine.

O World, George Santayana

Our Traveled Land

LEADER: We have placed the map of America by the flag Christopher Columbus planted in the earth of this land. We light this candle. It is with the light of faith that we venture forth across our land.

(pause)

As your name is called, come forward and place on our map your family sign for places you have traveled. Mark those places where relatives and friends now live.

(pause)

Let us listen to God's words of sending to a new land.

READER 2: "Go forth from the land of your kinsfolk and from your father's house to a land that I will show you. Abraham was seventy-five years old when he left his homeland. Abraham took his wife Sarah, his brother's son, Lot, all the possessions that they had accumulated and acquired and set out to the land of Canaan. When they arrived, Abraham pitched his tent and built an altar to the Lord and called the Lord by name."

Genesis 12:1, 4, 5, 7

This is the Word of the Lord.

ALL: Thanks be to God.

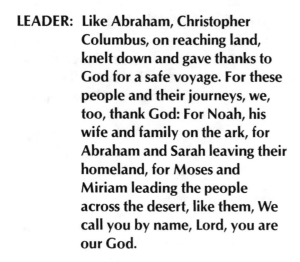

LEADER: Like Abraham, Christopher Columbus, on reaching land, knelt down and gave thanks to God for a safe voyage. For these people and their journeys, we, too, thank God: For Noah, his wife and family on the ark, for Abraham and Sarah leaving their homeland, for Moses and Miriam leading the people across the desert, like them, We call you by name, Lord, you are our God.

ALL: We call you by name, Lord, you are our God.

LEADER: For Isaiah, Jeremiah, Amos, and Jonah, prophets who traveled to towns, villages, cities, and countries, like them, We call you by name, Lord, you are our God.

ALL: We call you by name, Lord, you are our God.

LEADER: For fishermen Peter and Andrew, James and John, for disciples Paul, Timothy, Barnabas, Luke, for truth seekers Mary, Elizabeth, Magdalene, Martha, Anna, like them, We call you by name, Lord, you are our God.

ALL: We call you by name, Lord, you are our God.

LEADER: For explorers and missionaries, navigators and astronauts, for those journeying through outer space and the inner space of the heart, like them, We call you by name, Lord, you are our God.

ALL: We call you by name, Lord, you are our God.

LEADER: For our mothers, fathers, sisters, brothers, relatives, and friends, for each of us who have the courage to seek and reach beyond to mystery, like them, We call you by name, Lord, you are our God.

ALL: We call you by name, Lord, you are our God.

LEADER: Lord,
Give us light, your light for our journey. Instill in our hearts a deep faith in your presence in us and in our world. Protect and guide us on all paths we travel. We ask this in your name, Lord, our God.

ALL: Amen.

Rite of Journey

LEADER: We are all travelers on our planet Earth. God calls us and we respond. Whatever our choice, the traveled or untraveled path, we know God walks with us.

READER 3: Two roads diverged in a yellow wood, and sorry I
could not travel both and be one traveler,
Long I stood and looked down one as far as I could
to where it bent in the undergrowth;
Then took the other, as just as fair,
And having perhaps the better claim,
Because it was grassy and wanted wear;
Though as for that the pass there had worn them
really about the same,
And both that morning equally lay
In leaves no step had trodden black.
Oh, I kept the first for another day.
Yet knowing how way leads on to way,
I doubted if I should ever come back.
I shall be telling this with a sign
Somewhere ages and ages hence;
Two roads diverged in a wood, and I—
I took the one less traveled by,
And that had made all the difference.

Robert Frost, *The Road Not Taken*

LEADER: As a traveler on this planet earth, are you more likely to choose a worn and traveled path, or make your own path as you go?

(pause)

Think of the last time you had to make a choice in your direction in life? Was it easy? Hard?

(pause)

What path has made all the difference in your own life?

(pause)

In all our roads of life, let us praise the Lord.
Let us sing for joy to God who protects us.
Let us come before God with thanksgiving and make
a joyful noise with songs of praise.
Come, let us praise the Lord.

ALL: Come, let us praise the Lord.

LEADER: For the Lord is a great God, a mighty king
who rules over all the earth from the deepest
caves to the highest hills.
Come, let us praise the Lord.

ALL: Come, let us praise the Lord.

LEADER: God rules over the sea; God's hands farmed the dry land,
Come, let us worship and bow down before God
our maker. We are the people for whom God provides
and protects; we are the sheep of God's hand.
Come, let us praise the Lord.

ALL: Come, let us praise the Lord.

Psalm 95:1–5 (adapted)

Closing Blessing: Blessing for Travel

LEADER: God calls us to travel the known and unknown paths of life. With all explorers and navigators, missionaries, and seekers, we bow our head for God's blessing of light and faith. Lord, protect the way.

ALL: Protect the way.

LEADER: Lighten our traveling feet.

ALL: Lighten our traveling feet.

LEADER: Guide and direct our restless spirits.

ALL: Guide and direct our restless spirits.

LEADER: Answer the needs of our searching hearts.

ALL: Answer the needs of our searching hearts.

LEADER: Make safe all the roads of life.

ALL: Make safe all the roads of life.

LEADER: And make our journey, your journey, Lord.

ALL: And make our journey, your journey, Lord.

LEADER: And now as you go on your way:
May the road rise up to meet you.
May the wind be always at your back.
May the sun shine warm upon your face, the rains fall soft upon your fields.
And, until we meet again,
May you be held in the palm of God's hand.

An Irish Blessing

ALL: Amen.

Halloween

A Background Reflection

In the eighth century A.D., Gregory III had established the festival of All Saints Day (All Hallows) on November 1. In the next century, Gregory IV decreed the day to be a universal church observance in honor of all saints who died with or without church recognition of sanctity. On the next day (November 2), All Souls' Day, prayers are offered for the dead.

Medieval celebrations of New Year, May Day, Midsummer, and All Hallows shared similar festival activities. Centered around fire, the great medieval halls were decorated, mummers (bands of masked persons who danced in silence) performed, elaborate food was served, and games played. Presiding over the festivities were usually a king or queen for the evening. On All Hallows, someone dressed as King Crispin in regal robes with a large medallion on which was designed one big foot. This king—really St. Crispin—is the patron saint of shoemakers and cobblers. It is said that he preached all day and then worked with his hands all night, making shoes and giving praise to God in the very work he did.

These medieval Halloween festivals combined pagan customs of summer's end with Christian ones. Children wearing masks would go "souling" from door to door, singing and begging for soul cakes (flat, oval shortbread cookies with currants, cinnamon, and nutmeg) for wandering spirits. If no treats were offered, pranks were played.

Fire, a symbol of immortality among the ancients, was used on this night to welcome good spirits and prevent evil ones from coming near. Hollowed-out turnips, squash, or rutabagas were fashioned, with cut-out faces of grins or scowls. A lighted candle was placed inside. These were called Jack O'Lanterns. Irish legend says that a man named Jack was kept out of heaven because of his stinginess but not allowed to enter hell because of the jokes he played on the devil. So now he must roam the earth carrying a lantern. Pumpkins were first used after the discovery of America.

Children carried these jack o'lanterns to protect themselves from evil spirits and welcome good ones. Many farmers carried torches around the perimeter of fields, to scare away demons and protect crops while offering light to welcome the good spirits.

During October, supernatural beings were thought to be most powerful and lonely. They roamed the land as ghosts, fairies, elves, goblins, leprechauns, witches, and all kinds of supernatural beings. It became the custom of the day of Halloween to ask these spirits questions about love, life, and the identity of one's future spouse.

Apples were both used for fortune telling and for games. If you took an apple and pared it in one continuous length, twirled it around your head three times, and let it fall over your left shoulder, you would discover in the shape it took, the initials of your lover. Ducking for apples and biting at apples suspended from a string remain popular in America today.

Halloween in America today remains a favorite day for children but a worrisome one for parents. Communities have become concerned. With proper chaperoning and guidance, this holiday could offer an experience of treating property and people with respect as well as receiving treats from others. Many children carry UNICEF boxes and collect money for poor children of the world. This money goes to the United Nations fund and becomes a way of offering what we have to our less fortunate brothers and sisters around the world. In this way, we, indeed, become wandering spirits for others.

Preparations

directions

Hang the orange panel for the season of fall. Place a table before the panel and on it put smiling and frowning jack o'lanterns.

Choose three participants to place the three baskets on this table during prayer service.

Participants should have their jack o'lantern faces with them.

Choose tambourine players.

Choose someone to play King Crispin, and costume that person.

Have shoes for presenting.

Be prepared to call participants by name.

Choose two readers.

Three baskets should be filled with apples, nuts, and soul cakes.

materials

Construction paper
Scissors
Magic markers
Tambourines
Baskets
Apples, nuts, soul cakes
Table
Orange panel

Project

Make two one-dimensional jack o'lantern faces —one smiling, the other frowning. Cut out nose, eyes, mouth. Place a candle behind each. Or carve out two real pumpkins. Place a candle inside each.

Have each participant make a jack o'lantern face—either a smiling or a frowning one. Cut out.

Dress King Crispin in a robe. Make a large medallion with a shoe on it.

Make or buy small cakes (shortbread cookies).

Make a "shoe" for each participant of construction paper.

Prayer Celebration

Opening Greeting

LEADER: We gather together to celebrate the spirit of God alive within each of us. In this Spirit, we ask guidance and protection for all the days and nights of our life.

Light of Jack O'Lanterns

LEADER: This is the eve for merrymaking, the eve for lighting fire to welcome good spirits and to prevent not-so-good spirits from coming near. We light the candle of our smiling jack o'lantern and we say, "Lord, we are thankful." For the times we choose to walk happily and friendly in your light,

ALL: Lord, we are thankful.

LEADER: For the times we are able to see your light in the people we meet,

ALL: Lord, we are thankful.

LEADER: For the times we recognize your smiling light living deep in our heart,

ALL: Lord, we are thankful.

LEADER: We light the candle of our frowning jack o'lantern and we say, "Lord, we are sorry." For the times we walked with grumpy and frowning faces thinking only of ourselves,

ALL: Lord, we are sorry.

LEADER: For the times we closed our eyes to the needs of others,

ALL: Lord, we are sorry.

LEADER: For the times we did not live in your light,

ALL: Lord, we are sorry.

LEADER: We hold up our own jack o'lantern face. Through its smiles or frowns, the light of your spirit in us, Lord, continues to shine through for everyone to see.

(Everyone holds up jack o'lantern face.)

Lord,
we thank you for the light of your spirit, which continues to shine through all times so that together we bless ourselves in your presence.

ALL: In the name of the Father, and of the Son, and of the Holy Spirit. Amen.

The Journey Presentation

LEADER: To our celebration we welcome King Crispin, patron of shoemakers and all people who help our feet walk the height and depth, width and breadth of this earth.

(King Crispin arrives. Tambourines play.)

On our feast table, we place three baskets of food—
a basket of apples—

(Tambourines play.)

a basket of nuts—

(tambourines)

and a basket of soul cakes.

(tambourines)

Life is a journey. Where we are going and how we will get there are questions that life daily offers us. On this journey we know that we have God's protection and we need never walk alone. Let us listen to this scripture story, which tells of God's promise of protection as we walk this earth.

READER 1: "Jacob left Beersheba and started toward Haran. At sunset he came to a holy place and camped there. He lay down to sleep, resting his head on a stone. He dreamed that he saw a stairway reaching from earth to heaven, with angels going up and coming down on it. And there was the Lord standing beside him. 'I am the Lord, the God of Abraham and Isaac,' he said. 'I will give to you and to your descendants this land on which you are living. They will be as numerous as the specks of dust on the earth. They will extend their territory in all directions, and through you and your descendants, I will bless all nations. Remember, I will be with you and protect you wherever you go, and I will bring you back to this land.'"

Genesis 28:10–15 GNB

This is the Word of the Lord.

ALL: Thanks be to God.

LEADER: As your name is called, come forward and receive a sign of your willingness to walk this earth under God's protection. _____(Name)_____, know that God is with you.

(Pin paper shoe on each participant.)

Trick or Treat

LEADER: On Halloween night, we are all trick or treaters. Like the soulers of old, we wear our masks and ask for treats for our wandering spirits. We extend one hand before us as we circle the room.

(Tambourines play during chant.)

Souling, souling, for soul cakes we go,

ALL: Souling, souling, for soul cakes we go.

LEADER: One for Peter, two for Paul,

ALL: One for Peter, two for Paul.

LEADER: Three for him who made us all.

ALL: Three for him who made us all.

LEADER: If you haven't got a cake, an apple will do,

ALL: If you haven't got a cake, an apple will do.

LEADER: If you haven't got an apple, give a nut or two.

ALL: If you haven't got an apple, give a nut or two.

LEADER: If you haven't got a nut, then God bless you.

ALL: If you haven't got a nut, then God bless you.

(Chant and circle twice, wearing masks. As the chanters pass the head table during the second round, they are invited to take from the apple, nut, or soul cake baskets.)

We need never play tricks on others, for God is generous through the people who love and care for us.

A Closing Blessing: Blessing Before Travel on Halloween Night

LEADER: Let us listen to these words of scripture.

READER 2: **"Before setting out on his journey, the young Tobiah kissed his father and mother. His father Tobit said to him, 'Have a safe journey' and spoke comforting words to the worried mother— 'Our child leaves in good health and will come back to us in good health. Your own eyes will see his safe return. So, do not worry, my love. For a good spirit will go with him and he will return unharmed.'"**

Tobit 5:17–22 (adapted)

This is the Word of the Lord.

ALL: **Thanks be to God.**

LEADER: We ask God's blessing for each of us as we travel. Our response will be, "Lord, be with us." That you may safely walk the streets of your neighborhood,

ALL: Lord, be with us.

LEADER: That you may treat others kindly and not trick them by what you do or say,

ALL: Lord, be with us.

LEADER: That the Spirit protect and guide you and return you home in peace and joy.

ALL: Lord, be with us.

LEADER: Lord, God,
Guide our friends as they begin their journey. Bless them with peace as they travel and bring them home safely. Let us go forth in the peace and love of Christ and become his wandering spirits on this eve of All Hallows.

ALL: Amen.

World Peace Day

A Background Reflection

The vision of peace begins and develops through God's relationship with people. Founded on justice, peace is a result of God's loving and forgiving presence among us: "I am your God. You are my people. I love you. Love me. Love one another. Be my friend. Be the friend of others." Through the Hebrew scriptures, we understand this promise of love and friendship, and we discover that peace comes through fidelity to the covenant relationship.

In the Christian scriptures, we discover Jesus as God's peace. Through Jesus we continue to be formed and shaped as friends of God and one another. In his active love for all people, Jesus is the model of peacemaking and challenges us to become ministers of reconciliation as we allow God to change us from enemies into friends and become one with God and one with all that God has made.

On the last weekend in May 1983, over 10,000 Catholics, Protestants, and Jewish congregations in the United States participated in Peace Sabbath/Peace Sunday. The religious communities offered a new vision and hope for a world filled with God's peace and justice.

In 1981, the United Nations General Assembly had declared that the third Tuesday of September, the opening day of the regular sessions of the General Assembly, be designated and observed as International Day of Peace. Its intent was to strengthen the ideals of peace both within and among all nations and peoples. At this time, an International Year of Peace was proclaimed for 1986.

The Sunday nearest Armistice Day (November 11) has been designated as World Peace Sunday for Protestants of the National Council of Churches. This day is devoted to prayer for peace and a world without war.

In response to the call of Jesus to be peacemakers in our time and situation, the Catholic bishops wrote a pastoral letter entitled "The Challenge of Peace: God's Promise, Our Promise." In this letter they call for the disarmament of the human heart, for a conversion of the human spirit to God, for a new vision of the world as one interdependent planet. No longer is peacemaking seen as an optional commitment but rather as a requirement of faith. The letter said, "The work of building peace has just begun. The specific strategies for making peace will be the challenge of all men and women of good will." It is to this work that the document challenges us.

Every August 6, a Peace Festival is held at the Hiroshima Peace Park in memory of the victims of the August 6, 1945, atomic bomb explosion. In 1958, a statue of a young girl, Sadako, holding a peace crane in outstretched hands, was unveiled. Children from all over the world make these paper birds and send them to Japan on this day as their prayer for peace. (Send to World Friendship Center, 1544 Mirobimachi, Hiroshima, Japan.)

Sadako Sasaki, an active student and athlete by age 12, was two years old when the atom bomb was dropped. Ten years later, Sadako died as a result of radiation sickness from the bomb. Her story is told by Eleanor Coerr in *Sadako and the Thousand Paper Cranes* (Putnam Pub Group, 1977). It is a story of love and companionship offered this young girl by family, school, friends, and the community. In her life, Sadako offers us hope, vision, and a dream when all people can one day live in peace.

A Japanese tradition states that if one folds a thousand paper cranes, one's deepest wish will come true. With courage, this little girl began to fold cranes from her hospital bed. The more discouraged she became with her illness, the more determined she was in the folding of the cranes. With each crane came the yearning to be well again and the deepened hope that war would cease. Her prayer deep in her heart was "Little crane, I write peace on your wings and send you to fly over all the world." When Sadako died in 1955, she had folded 644 paper cranes.

The remaining 356 cranes were folded by her classmates, so that 1,000 cranes were buried with her. It is these same classmates and friends that collected money from children around the world to build a statue in her honor. Across the base of this statue, the Japanese children engraved these words:

This is our cry.

This is our prayer:

peace in the world.

Peacemakers come in all shapes and sizes. We can all be signs of peace. When people come in contact with us, they should know from our presence what peace, pardon, and love are about. Together, let us build a peaceable kingdom. John Paul II used this image: "Like a cathedral, peace must be constructed patiently and with unshakable faith." A more genuinely human world is not ensured by the absence of war, but rather in living together with the full awareness of the worth and dignity of every human person and of the sacredness of all human life. We seek to construct a world of peace and justice to ensure universal respect for the human rights and human dignity of every person. As citizens of the world, we make decisions for the good of the whole human family, and show compassion for the least important in that family, the hungry, thirsty, stranger, naked, ill, the imprisoned.

Let us plant ourselves as seeds of peace and by the way we live for others, let us nourish and grow as peacemakers, instruments of God's peace. Through the peace prayer of St. Francis, we sow love, bring pardon, faith, hope, light, and joy to our troubled and broken world. "Blessed are the peacemakers, for they shall be called children of God" (Matthew 5:9).

For more information on peace activities, please write to the following groups:

Clergy and Laity Concerned
198 Broadway
New York, NY 10038

Fellowship of Reconciliation
Box 271
Nyack, NY 10960

National Council of Churches
475 Riverside Dr.
New York, NY 10115

Commission on Social Action of Union of American Hebrew Congregations
2027 Massachusetts Ave. NW
Washington, DC 20036

Pax Christi (USA)
6337 West Cornelia
Chicago, IL 60634

Sojourners
Box 29272
Washington, DC 20017

World Peacemakers
2852 Ontario Rd. NW
Washington, DC 20009

Preparations

directions

Hang the orange panel for season of fall.

Make and place the peace tree on panel.

Place four candles—representing north, south, east, and west—before the panel. (If you have a Yule Wheel, use it at this time.)

Choose a reader and a storyteller.

Choose participants to place six signs from the Peace Prayer on Peace Tree during Prayer Celebration.

Each participant should have his or her "seed name" ready for presentation.

materials

Orange panel
Four candles (Yule Wheel, if you have one)
Construction paper
Magic markers
Scissors
Pins or glue

Project

Make a tree to represent the Peace Tree and place on orange panel.

Make "seeds." Have each participant place his or her name on one of these seeds.

Divide participants into six groups. Each group is responsible for making one sign for the Peace Prayer. On the back of each sign, group members write the ways they will work to achieve peace through

Love	(a heart)
Pardon	(a hand)
Faith	(a Chi-Rho)
Hope	(an anchor)
Light	(a candle)
Joy	(a smiling face)

Make a paper crane. (If you are sending cranes to Japan, then make agreed-upon number.)

Hope

Pardon

Joy

Faith

Peace Tree

Love

Light

Prayer Celebration

Opening Greeting

LEADER: Peace be with you.

ALL: And also with you.

LEADER: May the peace of Christ reign in your hearts.

ALL: And also in your heart.

LEADER: God's work is peace. As members of one body, we are called to plant seeds of peace and to nourish their growth by the way we live for others. We light our candles of peace. To God belongs the north,

(Light candle.)

the south,

(Light candle.)

the east,

(Light candle.)

the west.

(Light candle.)

Wherever we turn to pray, there is the face of God. May these lights of peace shine in the hearts of all God's peacemakers. As God's children we become the seeds of peace. We place our seed name below our tree of peace as a sign of our willingness to grow in peace.

(pause)

Blessed are the peacemakers for they shall be called children of God.

Matthew 5:9

ALL: Blessed are the peacemakers for they shall be called children of God.

The Word of God

LEADER: The words of Isaiah ask us to become a garden with a bubbling spring of water that never goes dry as we share and nourish others in peace.

READER 1: "Remove the chains of oppression and the yoke of injustice, and let the oppressed go free. Share your food with the hungry and open your homes to the homeless poor. Give clothes to those who have nothing to wear, and do not refuse to help your own relatives. Then my favor will shine on you like the morning sun and your wounds will be quickly healed. The darkness around you will turn to the brightness of noon. And I will always guide you and satisfy you with good things. I will keep you strong and well. You will be like a garden that has plenty of water, like a spring of water that never goes dry. Your people will rebuild what has long been in ruins. You will be known as the people who restored the ruined houses."

Isaiah 58:6–8, 10–12 (adapted)

This is the Word of the Lord.

ALL: Thanks be to God.

LEADER: Blessed are the peacemakers, for they shall be called children of God.

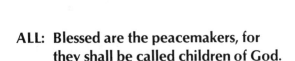

ALL: Blessed are the peacemakers, for they shall be called children of God.

Peace Prayer and Story

LEADER: Eight hundred years ago, Francis of Assisi wrote this prayer of peace. As instruments of God's peace, we become peacemakers of our world. Lord, make me an instrument of your peace, where there is hatred, let me sow love.

ALL: Where there is hatred, let me sow love.

LEADER: As we think of ways to rid our own hearts of bitterness, we place a sign of love on our Peace Tree.

(pause)

Where there is injury, let me bring pardon.

ALL: Where there is injury, let me bring pardon.

LEADER: As we think of ways to forgive ourselves and others, we place a sign of pardon on our Peace Tree.

(pause)

Where there is doubt, let me bring faith.

ALL: Where there is doubt, let me bring faith.

LEADER: As we think of ways to relieve doubt in ourselves and others, let us place a sign of faith on our Peace Tree.

(pause and do so)

Where there is despair, let me bring hope.

ALL: Where there is despair, let me bring hope.

LEADER: As we think of ways to dispel loneliness and fear, let us place a sign of hope on our Peace Tree.

(pause)

Where there is darkness, let me bring light.

ALL: Where there is darkness, let me bring light.

LEADER: As we think of ways to brush away gloom, let us place a sign of light on our Peace Tree.

(pause)

Where there is sadness, let me bring joy.

ALL: Where there is sadness, let me bring joy.

LEADER: As we think of ways to lift the hearts and spirits of ourselves and others, let us place a sign of joy on our Peace Tree.

(pause)

O, God, grant that we may never seek to be consoled as to console,

ALL: To be consoled as to console

LEADER: to be understood as to understand,

ALL: to be understood as to understand

LEADER: to be loved as to love

ALL: to be loved as to love

LEADER: For it is in giving that we receive,

ALL: For it is in giving that we receive,

LEADER: it is in pardoning that we are pardoned,

ALL: it is in pardoning that we are pardoned,

LEADER: and it is in dying that we are born to eternal life.

ALL: and it is in dying that we are born to eternal life.

STORY-TELLER: (tells the story of Sadako and the Japanese tradition of the 1,000 cranes)

LEADER: As we place our crane on our Peace Tree in honor of Sadako and all children everywhere as they work for peace, we pray this prayer in our hearts as Sadako once did with each crane she folded:
"Little Crane, I write peace on your wings and send you to fly over all the world."

(Pause—if you are sending cranes to Japan, make your offering at this time.)

Blessed are the peacemakers for they shall be called children of God.

ALL: Blessed are the peacemakers for they shall be called children of God.

Closing Blessing: Blessing of Peace

LEADER: Peacemakers come in all shapes and sizes. We give thanks to God for calling us to do the work of peace in our world today. Bow your head for God's blessing of peace. Be a maker of peace and make gentle the ways of this world.

ALL: Amen.

LEADER: Walk in peace. Work in peace. Live in Peace.

ALL: Amen.

LEADER: Be with another in peace. Be with yourself in peace.

ALL: Amen

LEADER: Be active as peace is active, in doing something
in making something
in becoming one with God and one
with all the people God has made

(Ikonographics, *Peace,* a Reflection Film)

ALL: Amen.

LEADER: In the words of Jesus, let us offer one another a blessing and sign of peace. Let us turn to each other and say, "My friend, I give you my peace."

ALL: "My friend, I give you my peace."

John 14:27

(Offer a sign of peace.)

Harvest Day

A Background Reflection

Since people first planted grain in the earth and watched it grow and ripen, there have been harvest festivals. We all seem to have a universal need to give thanks to our God for the fruits of the earth.

In Greece these festivals gave tribute to the grain goddess Demeter. Other countries addressed this goddess as "Mother of Grains," or "Mother of Fields." Ancient belief in this great Mother can be seen even today with the superstition accorded the last sheaf in every field. In France, the last sheaf is tied in the form of a cross, decorated with ribbons and flowers, and displayed in the home as a sign of blessing. In England we find the last sheaf being braided into a doll, dressed with flowers and ribbons, and displayed on a pole for all to see, or ceremoniously thrown into the river to ensure plenty of rain for next year's crops. In Austria, the last sheaf was shaped into a wreath and placed as a crown on the village girl designated as Harvest Queen. In Poland, the harvest wreaths decorated with flowers, apples, nuts, and ribbons are reminiscent of the one we see on doors or in people's homes today.

Our earliest roots in giving thanks come from Moses, instituting two great thanksgiving feasts among the Hebrews: Feast of Spring Harvest, Shavout, and the Feast of Fall Harvest, Sukkot. Sukkot represents the fresh start of a new year and the same time the harvest of the old year. It is a holiday to celebrate all growing plants. During this weeklong festival, a booth or hut, a *sukkah* was built. The Book of Leviticus describes the manner in which a *sukkah* was constructed: three walls, a branch-covered roof with an opening to the sky. This opening allowed the stars to be seen and rain to be received, both reminding the people of God beyond. The *sukkah* is decorated with fruits and vegetables.

This dwelling in booths probably originated as a temporary dwelling for harvesters to finish work in the field without having to journey home; they are also symbolic of the makeshift dwellings the people made as they wandered in the desert for forty years. These booths remind us of a simpler life, closer to nature. As symbols, they suggest that life, though precarious and transient, is still filled with richness, color, and joy. The tabernacle in Christian churches, is a direct descendant of the tabernacle, tent, or *sukkah* that was the first holy dwelling in the wilderness.

New England pilgrims who commemorated their harvest with a feast of Thanksgiving probably used Sukkot as a model. For these pilgrims, who had survived their first bitter winter, their first harvest was a time for rejoicing. The Indians had shared their seeds of corn (maize). When the corn was harvested, there was celebration and thanksgiving. For the Indians gathered at this Thanksgiving feast, it was a reminder of their own harvest celebration for the previous hundreds of years. This Pilgrim Thanksgiving and the foods served then became the pattern for our present Thanksgiving—turkey, apple cider, pumpkin pie, nuts, and an abundance of all the fruits of autumn. In all fifty states, Thanksgiving is now celebrated on the fourth Thursday in November; in Canada, on the second Monday in October.

The autumnal equinox that marks the official change of season is situated halfway between the summer and winter solstice. On this day the sun crosses the equator from north to south. For the Northern Hemisphere, this date is usually September 23. On this day, as with the vernal equinox of March 21, day and night are of equal length. So we have three things in common with our brothers and sisters around the planet Earth at this time of the year—the experience of equal day and night, the wonder in our hearts as we gather to partake of the abundance produced by the good earth at harvest, and the call to share that plenty with those in need.

The season of autumn has always played a vivid role in the life of the farmer. Autumn remains the period of harvest, vintage, and fruit gathering. The harvest moon—the full moon nearest the time of the equinox—appears above the horizon at about sunset for a number of days and provides light for farmers to harvest into the night. Americans call this season fall, which means the time when the red and golden leaves fall from trees. Autumn can be sad, because summer and outdoor living is over, but it is also a happy time, because it is the season of harvest. Many people of the world, whose calendars differ from ours, now celebrate their New Year. For them the autumn also reflects the two moods, joy for a new year's beginning and sadness for the old year's end. But, always, permeating both moods, is the need to say thanks for all gifts great and small.

Preparations

directions

Hang the orange panel for the autumn season horizontally—this will suggest the *sukkah*.

Define the space of your *sukkah* before the orange panel. Explain what a *sukkah* is and how and why it was constructed.

Alert the participants that they will be called by name during the prayer service to gather and sit in this *sukkah*.

Choose one reader.

Choose four people to present the autumn fruits, seeds, bread, and juice that will be placed in the center of the gathering.

materials

Fruits, seeds, bread, juice
Decorations for the *sukkah*—branches, leaves, vegetables, streamers, etc.

Project

Make a *sukkah* (tentlike dwelling). Be as elaborate as you wish or simply use the orange panel draped horizontally. Decorate with fall leaves, corn husks, wheat sheafs, grapes, autumn vegetables, and fruits.

Prayer Celebration

Opening Greeting

LEADER: Autumn is the season of gathering, a time of harvest. In thanksgiving, we bow our heads in gratitude for all God's blessings. In praise we rejoice in the goodness of life. The Lord be with you.

ALL: And also with you.

LEADER: Lift up your hearts.

ALL: We lift them up to the Lord.

LEADER: Let us give thanks to the Lord our God.

ALL: It is right to give God thanks and praise.

The Gathering Call

LEADER: At the time of the autumnal equinox, the position of the sun offers to every place on earth, equal length of day and night. To all places, east and west, north and south, the call goes out to gather together the harvest of the earth and the people of the harvest:
Come, _____ (Names) _____ welcome to the dwelling place of the Lord.

(Call participants in groups of four to take their place in the sukkah.)

And to this dwelling place of the Lord we bring the harvest of the earth. We bring the autumn fruits and say, "Thank you, Lord, for the harvest of your earth."

ALL: Thank you, Lord, for the harvest of your earth.

LEADER: We bring autumn seeds and say, "Thank you, Lord, for the harvest of your earth."

ALL: Thank you, Lord, for the harvest of your earth.

LEADER: We bring sheafs of autumn grains made into bread, and say, "Thank you, Lord, for the harvest of your earth."

ALL: Thank you, Lord, for the harvest of your earth.

LEADER: We bring autumn grapes made into wine, and say, "Thank you, Lord, for the harvest of your earth."

ALL: Thank you, Lord, for the harvest of your earth.

The Gathered

LEADER: And we ask, why do we gather together? Why do we come to this pilgrim feast of the Lord? Why do we give thanks? And for our answers we listen with our hearts to God's word to us in scripture.

READER 1: "The Lord said to Moses. Speak to the Israelites and tell them: There are many festivals of the Lord, my feast days, which I ask you to celebrate with a sacred assembly. At one of these, the Feast of Booths, I ask you to gather the produce of the land and celebrate for a week a pilgrim feast of the Lord. On the first day gather branches of palms, myrtles, and poplars and make merry before the Lord your God. During this week, I ask you to dwell in booths, that your descendants may realize that when I led the Israelites out of the land of Egypt, I made them dwell in booths. I, the Lord, am your God."

Leviticus 23:1, 2, 34, 39–43 (adapted)

This is the Word of the Lord.

ALL: **Thanks be to God.**

LEADER: **We are a sacred people for the Lord dwells among us and within us. In this gathering place, we celebrate as a sacred assembly. Here in our booth we make merry before the Lord. Through our opening to the sky, we welcome sun, moon, stars, all God's gifts, and we say,**

ALL: **It is right to give God thanks and praise.**

Psalm 92:2

LEADER: **With tree branches, fruits, and vegetables of the harvest, all God's gifts, we say,**

ALL: **It is right to give God thanks and praise.**

LEADER: **With colored leaves, signs of the changing season, all God's gifts, we say,**

ALL: **It is right to give God thanks and praise.**

LEADER: **With sheafs and bread, grapes and wine, all God's gifts, we say,**

ALL: **It is right to give God thanks and praise.**

LEADER: **From our Hebrew traditions and heritage, we now bless these gifts:**

(Take bread and hold it.)

Blessed are you, Lord our God, king of the universe,

ALL: **Blessed are you, Lord our God, king of the universe,**

LEADER: **who gives to us bread,**

ALL: **who gives to us bread,**

LEADER: **and causes the earth to overflow with good for all.**

ALL: **and causes the earth to overflow with good for all.**

(Pass bread; take the wine [juice] and hold it.)

LEADER: **Blessed are you, Lord our God, king of the universe,**

ALL: **Blessed are you, Lord our God, king of the universe,**

LEADER: **who from the vine has created the gift of wine,**

ALL: **who from the vine has created the gift of wine,**

LEADER: **a sign of our love and unity.**

ALL: **a sign of our love and unity.**

(Pass wine; take the seeds and hold them.)

LEADER: Blessed are you, Lord our God, king of the universe,

ALL: Blessed are you, Lord our God, king of the universe,

LEADER: who gives us seedtime and harvest,

ALL: who gives us seedtime and harvest,

LEADER: a sign of your faithful presence within us and all creation.

ALL: a sign of your faithful presence within us and all creation.

(Pass seeds.)

LEADER: Lord,
You are our God, our creator. You sustain us with your life. Give us hearts that rejoice in the wondrous gifts of the earth. Give us hands that share these gifts with all those in need wherever they may be. This harvest reveals your goodness, Lord. As people of the harvest, continue to gather us and all creation into your shelter of peace where we will dwell with you forever.

ALL: Amen.

Closing Blessing

LEADER: As a gesture of thanks, we stand, raise our heads, and open our hands in gratitude to the Lord, our God.
The earth has yielded its fruits; God our God has blessed us.

Psalm 67:7

ALL: Amen.

LEADER: God made the moon to mark the seasons and
the sun to know the hour of its setting.

Psalm 104:19

ALL: Amen.

LEADER: Many will gather from the east and west and will find a place in the banquet in the kingdom of God.

Matthew 8:11

ALL: Amen.

LEADER: Let us go forth as God's gathering people and share the richness of the harvest with all God's creation.

ALL: So be it. So be it. So be it.

LEADER: To our home meals we now bring our loaves of bread. Share them with your family and symbolically with all God's people. With the crumbs, feed the birds, as a sign that our hands care for all God's creation.

ALL: Together we ask God to daily give us bread to eat through the prayer Jesus taught us:
OUR FATHER, WHO ART IN HEAVEN, HALLOWED BE YOUR NAME, YOUR KINGDOM COME, YOUR WILL BE DONE ON EARTH AS IT IS IN HEAVEN. GIVE US THIS DAY OUR DAILY BREAD AND FORGIVE US OUR TRESPASSES AS WE FORGIVE THOSE WHO TRESPASS AGAINST US. AND LEAD US NOT INTO TEMPTATION BUT DELIVER US FROM EVIL. FOR YOURS IS THE KINGDOM AND THE GLORY NOW AND FOREVER. AMEN.

Advent

A Background Reflection

Advent is a season in the Church year that gives us time to wait for something to happen. During four, usually long, weeks we anticipate Christ coming into our lives in a special way at Christmas.

We wait expectantly and joyfully for Christmas. We often wait in our lives. We wait for people we plan to meet, wait at the doctor's office, wait for the bus to come, for vacation to begin, for our birthday to arrive. The Advent season gives us the opportunity to reflect on the way we live while waiting. This is the time to prepare for the awaited event of Christmas.

The word *advent* means coming. During Advent we not only remember Jesus' first coming into our world at his birth, but we also celebrate his daily comings into our hearts now and anticipate his future coming at the end of time. These comings represent different aspects of the presence of God in our lives throughout all time.

The Advent wreath and the Jesse tree symbols help us to remember during Advent that all people of all times have awaited the coming of the Messiah. We join with them as one people making ready the way of the Lord. As a family or class, choose the ways in which you will prepare for the renewal of Christmas.

One way to await Jesus' birthday is to pray or sing the *O Antiphons* from the 9th century or earlier. The prayer celebration that follows is based on these antiphons. The hope-filled themes of the *O Antiphons* come mainly from the prophet Isaiah. In these antiphons, Jesus is awaited under different messianic titles: O Wisdom (Sapientia), My Lord (Adonai), Root of Jesse (Radix), Key of David (Clavis), Rising Sun (Oriens), King (Rex), God with us (Emmanuel). When read backward, the beginning letter of each title makes an acrostic *ERO CRAS*, which means "I will be tomorrow."

In the prayer service which follows, each *O Antiphon* is divided into three parts. Each antiphon begins with a title. Words praising Jesus and elaborating the meaning of the title follow. Then each antiphon concludes with a petition.

Preparation

directions

Complete the project.

Choose participants to carry the O-Antiphon symbols and to hang them in a window, or from the ceiling at staggered heights, during the celebration. (Save the symbols to use as Christmas-tree decorations.)

Choose a leader.

Choose a participant to ring bells during the Litany of Announcement.

Practice singing "O Come, O Come, Emmanuel."

materials

construction paper in a variety of colors
crayons and/or felt-tipped pens
ribbon or string
tacks

Project

Have the participants make two-sided, construction-paper symbols similar to those below for each O Antiphon. Attach a ribbon or string to the top of each symbol.

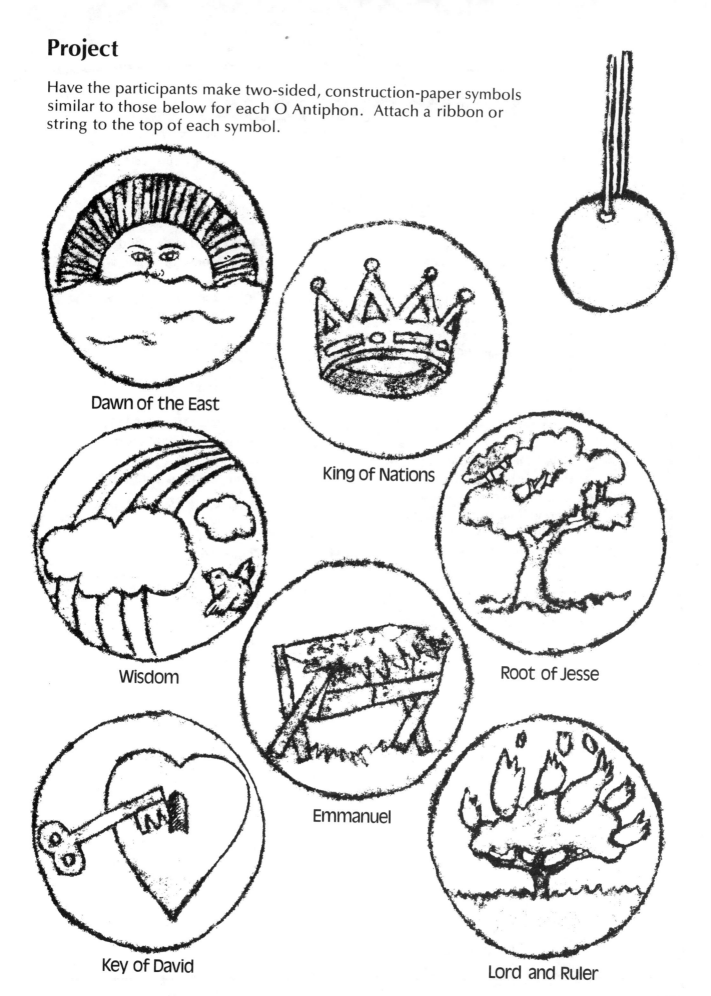

Dawn of the East

King of Nations

Wisdom

Root of Jesse

Emmanuel

Key of David

Lord and Ruler

Prayer Celebration

Introduction

LEADER: Together we are making ready the way of the Lord. We prepare for his coming into our lives at Christmas, we acknowledge his daily coming into our hearts, and we await his coming at the end of time. Like David and Isaiah, like all the prophets, like John the Baptist, we say, "Come, Lord Jesus, come."

The O Antiphons

LEADER: O WISDOM, who came from the mouth of the Most High, who reaches from end to end, who gives order to all things mightily and sweetly, Come and show us your Wisdom.

(The selected participant hangs up the Wisdom symbol.)

ALL: Come and show us your Wisdom.

LEADER: O LORD AND RULER of the House of Israel, who came to Moses in the burning bush, who gave to Moses the law on Mount Sinai, Come and redeem us.

(The selected participant hangs up the Lord-and-Ruler symbol.)

ALL: Come and redeem us.

LEADER: O ROOT OF JESSE, standing as a sign for all people, standing before the silence of kings, to whom the gentiles offer their prayers, Come and deliver us.

(The selected participant hangs up the Root-of-Jesse symbol.)

ALL: Come and deliver us.

LEADER: O KEY OF DAVID and Scepter of the House of Israel, who opens and no one closes, who closes and no one opens, Come and free us.

(The selected participant hangs up the Key-of-David symbol.)

ALL: Come and free us.

LEADER: O DAWN OF THE EAST, the brightness of light eternal, the Sun of justice, Come, bring us your light.

(The selected participant hangs up the Dawn-of-the-East symbol.)

ALL: Come, bring us your light.

LEADER: O KING OF NATIONS, the desired one, our cornerstone, you who will bring all people together, Come, make us one.

(The selected participant hangs up the King-of-Nations symbol.)

ALL: Come, make us one.

LEADER: O EMMANUEL, our King and Ruler, you are the expected one of all people, the savior for all nations, Come and save us.

(The selected participant hangs up the Emmanuel symbol.)

ALL: Come and save us.

LEADER:	Let us think of ways we welcome and prepare for Jesus' coming into our lives.
	(Pause.)
ALL:	(Sing "O Come, O Come, Emmanuel.")

The Litany of Announcement

LEADER:	Like Mary, we receive the greeting of the Lord and say yes to having Jesus in our lives.

(The selected participant rings the bell throughout the prayer, pausing slightly between each ring.)

	The angel Gabriel was sent from God to a town of Galilee named Nazareth. Greetings to you Mary, O favored one. The Lord is with you.
ALL:	And also with you.
LEADER:	Blessed are you among women! Do not be afraid, Mary. The Lord is with you.
ALL:	And also with you.
LEADER:	You have found favor with God. You shall conceive and bear a son and give him the name Jesus. The Lord is with you.
ALL:	And also with you.

LEADER:	The Holy Spirit will come on you, and God's power will rest upon you. The Lord is with you.
ALL:	And also with you.
LEADER:	The holy child will be called the Son of God. He will be great and his kingdom shall never end. The Lord is with you.
ALL:	And also with you.

(adapted from Luke 1:26–35)

Closing Prayer

LEADER:	Together, we prepare and wait for your coming, Lord, and we say, Come, Lord Jesus, Come. Like Mary and all of creation, we bow our heads and receive the blessing of God and the blessing of one another.
	May the Lord bless you and keep you.
ALL:	Amen.
LEADER:	May the light of the Lord shine on you and be gracious to you.
ALL:	Amen.
LEADER:	May the face of the Lord be shown to you and give you peace.
ALL:	Amen.
LEADER:	And as you wait for the coming of the Lord, make your hearts ready to welcome him.
ALL:	Come, Lord Jesus, Come!

St. Nicholas

A Background Reflection

On December 6, the children's festival of St. Nicholas is observed, primarily in Europe. Nicholas was born in a province of Asia Minor in the fourth century and grew up to become bishop of Myra. What little we know of his life comes to us through legends, which show him to be a generous man. Once he apparently gave three bags of gold to a poor man so that the man's three daughters would have dowries to marry.

In Greece, many ships sailed with an icon of Nicholas on board. Before the sailors put out to sea, they celebrated a service of St. Nicholas in which kollyva (boiled wheat grain) was blessed. Then, in rough wind, they threw either the kollyva or the icon into the sea to calm the wind.

Northern Europeans represent Nicholas as a tall, kind-faced man with a long white beard, wearing a cape, and carrying a staff. He rides a white horse followed by a cart full of parcels to be left at different homes. Children have stuffed their shoes with hay so the horse will have something to eat. St. Nicholas leaves candy and small gifts in place of the hay.

Many families in Europe used to welcome a representative of St. Nicholas into their homes on December 5th. This representative, dressed as a bishop, talked with the children and reminded them to prepare for the coming of Jesus at Christmas. Later, some people began giving Nicholas the name Father Christmas, or Santa Claus.

According to an ancient Advent custom in Europe, Canada, and South America, children placed little notes, addressed to the Child Jesus, on their window sills on December fifth. These notes told of their desired Christmas gifts. (Our family tells what we will do to prepare for Christmas.) St. Nicholas acts as a messenger to God. (We leave a heart in place of the letter after we gather them that night.)

St. Nicholas Day gives us a way to celebrate charity and to reflect on our ability to give without expecting something in return. God gave us Jesus as a gift. Through our gift of life, we are called to become a gift for others.

> There is more happiness in giving than in receiving.

Acts 20:35

Preparation

directions

Complete the projects.

Have the participants write letters to God stating what they will do to prepare themselves as gifts to God and others for Christmas. Place these letters in the participants' construction-paper shoes and line the shoes up on window sills in your home or classroom.

Choose a leader and someone to play St. Nicholas.

Without telling the story before the celebration, acquaint the participants with their responses in the play — "Oh, no!" "Oh, yes!" Applause. Tell them that the leader will nod his or her head when they are to respond.

Practice singing as a round the following words to the tune of "Row, Row, Row Your Boat":

> Give, give, give, give, give your heart to God. Happily, happily, happily, happily give your heart to God.

Optional: Bake Speculatius (St. Nicholas cookies from Holland) to eat after the celebration.

1 cup butter	4 tsp. cinnamon
1 cup lard	½ tsp. nutmeg
2 cups brown sugar	½ tsp. cloves
½ cup sour cream	4½ cups sifted flour
½ tsp. soda	½ cup chopped nuts

Cream butter, lard, sugar. Add sour cream alternately with sifted dry ingredients. Stir in nuts. Knead dough and form into rolls. Wrap rolls in waxed paper and chill in refrigerator overnight. Roll thin. Cut into shapes of St. Nicholas. Bake in moderate oven 10-15 minutes.

materials

construction paper in assorted colors
scissors
crayons or felt-tipped pens
paste or glue

Projects

Have the participants use the following pattern to make St. Nicholas figures. Before the celebration, give all the figures to "St. Nicholas" to use in the Letter Ceremony.

Have the participants use the following
pattern to make construction-paper shoes.
(If you prefer, the participants may use
their own shoes.)

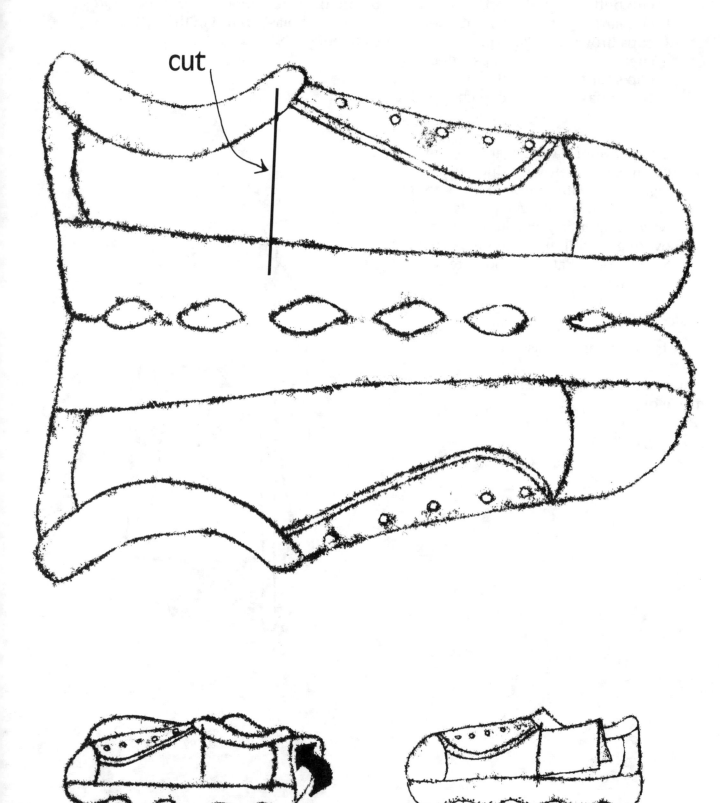

cut

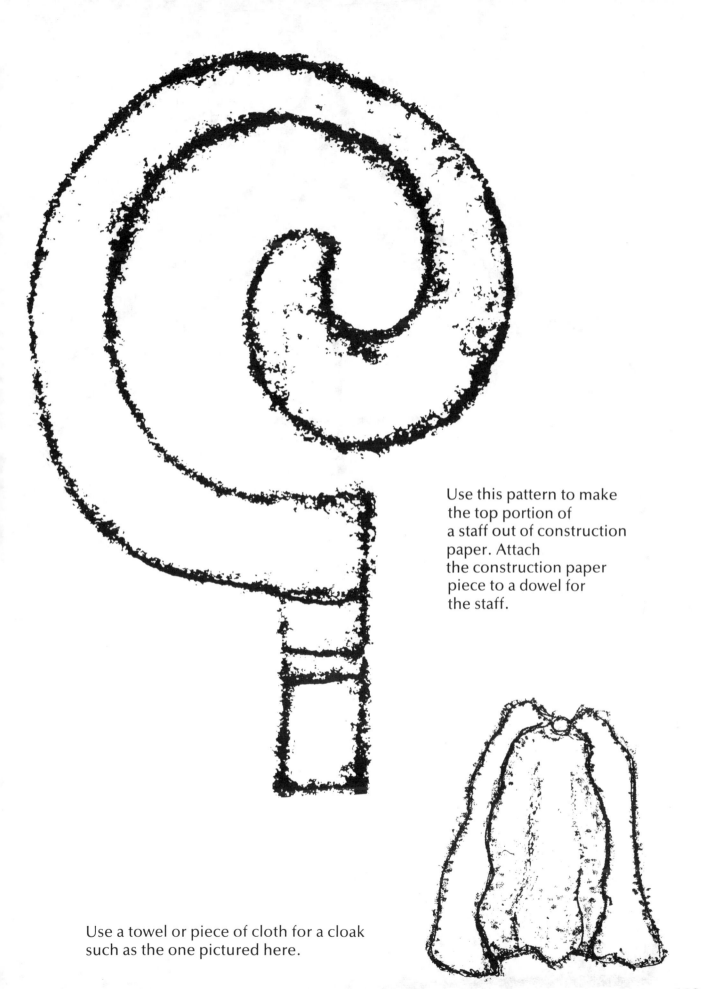

Use this pattern to make
the top portion of
a staff out of construction
paper. Attach
the construction paper
piece to a dowel for
the staff.

Use a towel or piece of cloth for a cloak
such as the one pictured here.

123

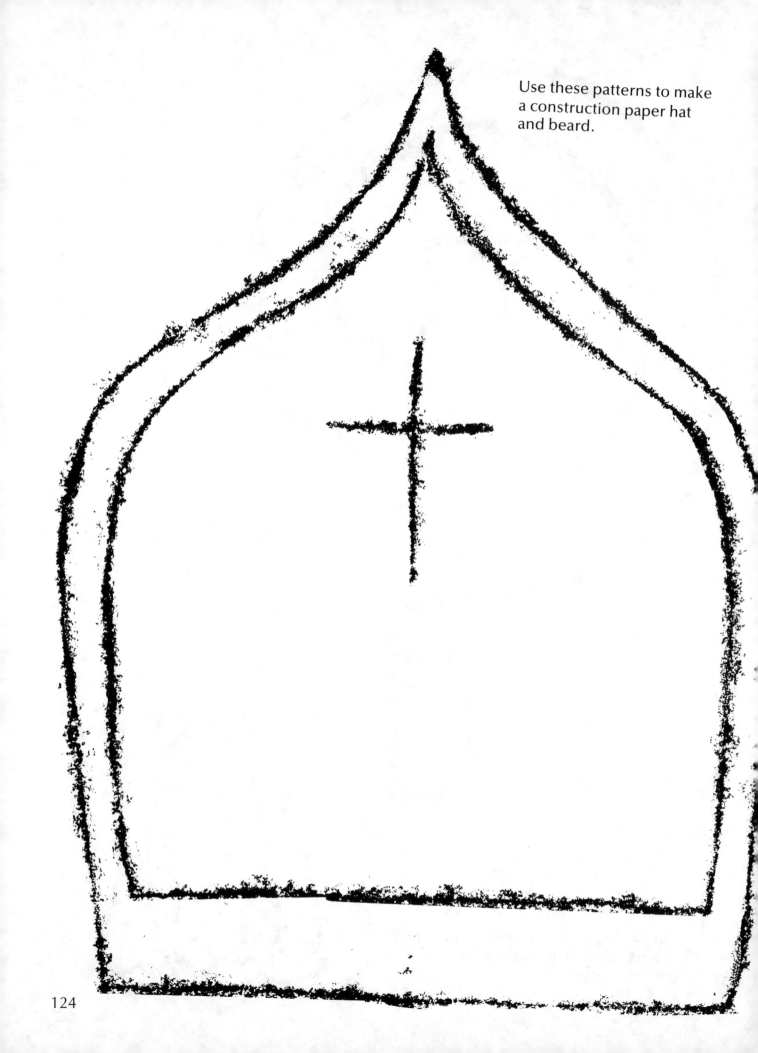

Use these patterns to make a construction paper hat and beard.

124

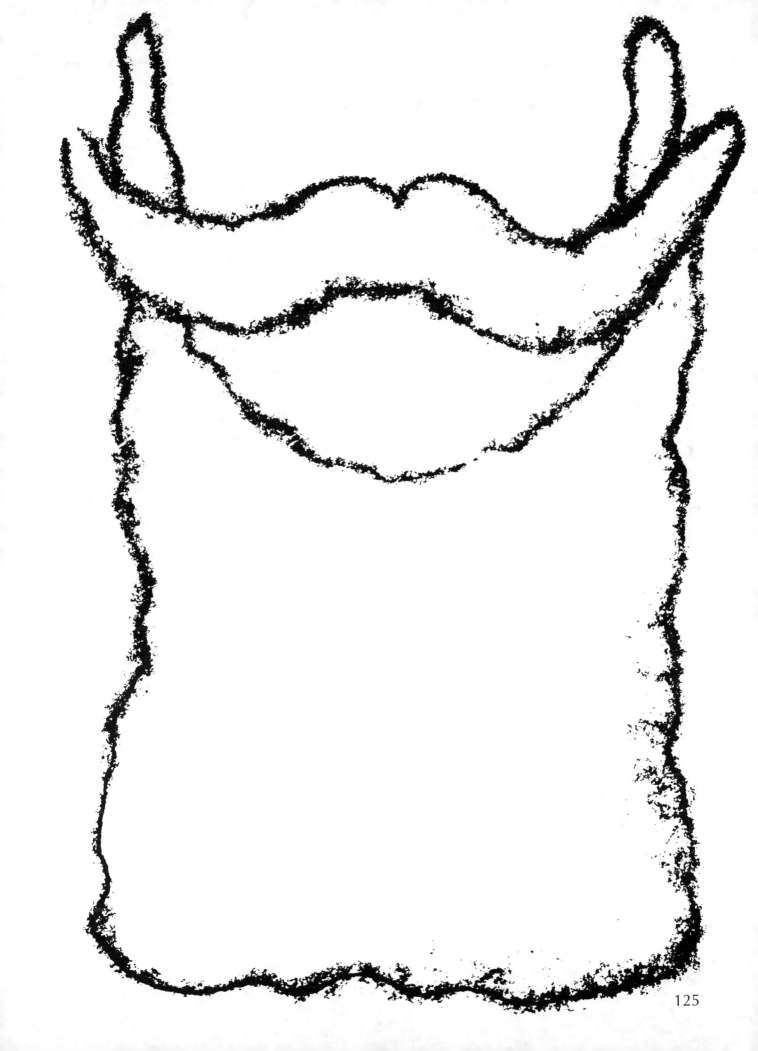

Prayer Celebration

Introduction

LEADER: Today we gather to celebrate giving gifts, gifts of being and doing for others. St. Nicholas teaches us through his life that we should share with everyone. Let us think of the ways we are preparing for the coming of Jesus at Christmas.

Are we praying? (Pause.)

Are listening to others?

Are we remembering that our talents, our families, our minds, our faith, our feelings, our very goodness comes from God? (Pause.)

Are we thanking? (Pause.)

Are we loving? (Pause.)

Are we giving? (Pause.)

Let us welcome Nicholas as a friend and listen to his story.

The Story of Cantalbert's Gift

NICHOLAS: My dear boys and girls, men and women, I want to tell you a story, a story of a young man called Cantalbert. Before he became a monk, Cantalbert was a juggler. He was an unhappy juggler, though, for no one paid him any attention. People laughed at him. He was a failure.

In the monastery, he could do nothing right. He tried to cook.

ALL: Oh, no!

NICHOLAS: He tried to copy manuscripts.

ALL: Oh, no!

NICHOLAS: He tried to paint frescoes.

ALL: Oh, no!

NICHOLAS: He tried to teach children, to write poetry, to sculpt, to compose music.

ALL: Oh, no!

NICHOLAS: Everyone complained.

ALL: Oh, no!

NICHOLAS: One day, it began to snow. Christmas was drawing near. All the brothers went to their rooms and prepared their Christmas gifts to give Mary and the Child Jesus.

The writers wrote.

ALL: Oh, yes!

NICHOLAS: The stone carvers carved.

ALL: Oh, yes!

NICHOLAS: The cook cooked.

ALL: Oh, yes!

NICHOLAS: The composer composed and the painter painted.

ALL: Oh, yes!

NICHOLAS: But Cantalbert did not know what to do. He thought and thought. Weeks went by and he thought some more. Finally Christmas arrived. Everyone went to the chapel to present their gifts.

The cook was first to present his gift — a wonderful cake. (Applause.)

Brother Martin read a moving poem he had written in Latin. (Applause.)

Brother Arnold presented a very tiny but perfect Bible which he had copied. (Applause.)

Brother Gerard sang the song which he had composed. (Applause.)

Brother Ernest gave a beautiful picture he had painted, and Brother Thomas presented an ivory statue he had carved. (Applause.)

But Cantalbert had nothing he could give. That night, when all the other monks were sleeping, Cantalbert tiptoed into the chapel. There, alone in the dark, he juggled all night to entertain Mary and her Son.

When morning came, the brothers hurried to the chapel as they always did. There they saw Cantalbert juggling.

ALL: Oh, no!

NICHOLAS: They saw him fall to the ground exhausted.

ALL: Oh, no!

NICHOLAS: They talked with one another. What should they do? As they turned to look at Cantalbert, they saw a rose next to him, the very same rose that had once rested in the hand of the statue of Mary. As they looked at the statue of Mary, there was a smile on her face. Cantalbert had given his gift to Mary, his very best gift, the gift of himself. (Applause.)

The Letter Ceremony

(During this ritual, sing as a round the following words to the tune of "Row, Row, Row Your Boat": Give, give, give, give, give your heart to God. Happily, happily, happily, happily give your heart to God.)

NICHOLAS: Prepare for the coming of Jesus into your hearts. I will take the letters you have written and place them in prayer before God.

(Each participant brings his or her shoe to Nicholas, who takes the letter out and places a St. Nicholas figure inside.)

Closing Prayer

LEADER: I give you now to the Lord. I have never wished I had someone else's silver or gold. Nor was I jealous of other people's clothes. Instead I have kept busy tending to my own needs and the needs of others. It is hard work helping other people, but Jesus told us, "It is better to give than to receive."

(adapted from Acts 20:32-35)